# THE CAMPFIRE COOKBOOK

## THE COMPLETE GUIDE TO EATING WELL IN THE WILD

# THE CAMPFIRE COOKBOOK

## THE COMPLETE GUIDE TO EATING WELL IN THE WILD

DON AND PAM PHILPOTT

This Wind-up Books edition published by Elwin Street Productions



Conceived and produced by
Elwin Street Limited
3 Percy Street
London W1T 1DE
United Kingdom
www.elwinstreet.com



ISBN 978-1-906761-75-2

10 9 8 7 6 5 4 3 2 1

# Contents

# INTRODUCTION

Every year, the pace of life gets faster, road traffic gets more congested and the pressures of urban living grow more intense. It isn't surprising, therefore, that more and more people escape to the great outdoors to get away from the crowds and the daily rush in search of fresh air and exercise and their own peace and quiet. In Great Britain alone more than six million people regularly walk in the Scottish, Welsh and English national parks and countryside.

Fortunately there are still huge tracts of country and wilderness to explore, from mountains and moors to crags and coastlines. There are tens of thousands of miles of long distance trails and bridle paths and cycle tracks. There is also a constantly changing environment as every season provides new panoramas and challenges. You can get so much more satisfaction from your trips if you are able to identify the birds, trees and flowers that you see along the way. You will appreciate it even more if you can recognize animal tracks and different geological formations.

However, you don't have to hike for days to enjoy the great outdoors, although this is certainly the best way to explore very remote countryside. Just spending a few hours away from urban living and the television can be enough to recharge your batteries. Exercise is another wonderful benefit, although the majority of people who venture into the hills claim to do so because they love it and not purely because of a desire to get fit. There are also many other pluses and food is one of them. The finest restaurant in the world cannot give you a view as stunning as that from the top of a mountain that you have just climbed. No gastro-pub can produce a meal as satisfying as the fish you have just caught and cooked. And who knows why, but coffee always tastes so much better when you sip it by the campfire underneath the stars.

Very few outdoor enthusiasts go walking or cycling just for the meal at the end of their day's exertions, but a good meal can really cap off a great day. Over the last few years, there have been enormous strides in the development of camping equipment and especially in lightweight stoves and accessories. Cooking in the open is actually a pleasure and an opportunity to enjoy some great cuisine with good friends in wonderful surroundings. The aim of this book is to encourage you to be adventurous in your approach to campside cooking. You don't have to rely on a can of beans for every meal or eat only dehydrated foods.

For many years, we were members of a backpackers' club that held an annual competition to see who could produce the finest gourmet meal on a single camping gas stove. The meal had to consist of four courses. Two prizes were awarded – one for the best campsite menu and one for the best meal cooked at the highest altitude. It was amazing how adventurous and how creative people were when cooking on peaks and hillsides at 3,000 m (10,000 feet) and higher.

While most of us will not have to go to such heights to follow that example, there is absolutely no reason why your results should not be just as mouth-watering. With the right ingredients you can eat in style and as you recognise more wild plants, you will be able to add fresh herbs, leaves, fungi and other edibles to enhance your dishes. With a little planning and the right cooking equipment, you can create meals that are exciting and delicious as well as healthy and nutritious.

Enjoy!

# CHAPTER ONE

## WAY TO GO

Most people visiting the countryside still prefer to walk. They may drive to a valley head or a parking spot but they then get out and walk. If they are out for just a few hours, they carry a day sack with wet-weather gear and a few essentials, including some food. If they are hiking into wild and remote country they use a large pack to carry everything they need for the duration of their trip. This is where skill is needed in selecting the right gear because you don't want to have to carry more weight than is absolutely necessary. Modern equipment, including stoves and cooking utensils, is light and it is not necessary to compromise on quality.

If you are cycling off road, you can carry a little more gear in panniers but again weight is a critical consideration. However, if you are one of the growing army of off-roaders with a 4x4 vehicle, weight is not a problem and you can pack a full-size camping grill if you want to. Even if you are only out for a day there is no reason why you shouldn't park somewhere that has a fabulous view, get out the grill and cook up a feast before heading back.

In many countries in the world, pony trekking is very popular. Riders can roam the open countryside while most of their gear is carried by pack horses. It is surprising how much equipment you can carry in this way so when you stop to make camp, you should have everything you need to prepare a great meal.

# LEAVE ONLY FOOTPRINTS

National parks and wilderness areas are a universal asset to be protected for future generations. Everyone therefore who enjoys the outdoors must be a conservationist, enjoying it to the full and minimising impact. In recent years, millions of acres of forest and natural country have been devastated by fire, homes destroyed and lives lost because of wild fires. Most authorities issue regulations and warnings about fire hazards. Never light fires where the danger levels are high.

There is always a responsibility to others to be prepared. If you are heading into the bush or the mountains, or plan to be away for a few days, make sure you have the right gear and adequate supplies, that you know how to use a map and compass, first aid, how to light the stove, and have checked the weather forecast. Above all, make sure someone knows about your plans and when you are due back.

A discarded cigarette butt takes up to five years to totally degrade. Banana peel takes three to five weeks, newspaper two to four weeks and a disposable diaper between 10 and 20 years. Hard plastic containers can take up to 30 years to degrade, a rubber soled boot up to 80 years, an aluminum can up to 400 years and a plastic six-pack holder up to 450 years. That is why we shouldn't litter the countryside and why if we pack it in, we should pack it out.

## ON THE TRAIL

Remember not to cause damage and don't litter even by accident. It is very easy to pull your hand out of your pocket and accidentally drop a wrapper or piece of paper. Keep a plastic bag in your pocket and use it to collect your trash. Also be a good guardian of the countryside and pick up trash left behind by those less considerate.

### IN AN EMERGENCY

**S** Stop and take stock.
**T** Think each step through before acting.
**O** Observe your supplies, surroundings and capabilities.
**P** Prioritise what's to be done and then follow the plan.

Natural objects of beauty or interest such as antlers, petrified wood, or colored rocks add to the mood of the backcountry and should also be left so others can experience a sense of discovery. In U.S. National Parks and some other areas it is illegal to remove natural objects. Even picking a few flowers can have a more significant impact than you may think. It is acceptable to gather a modest amount of fruits, berries and nuts for personal consumption provided you do not damage the remainder of the plant in the process.

Don't get too close to the wildlife so as not to disturb them. Watch from a distance using binoculars and take photographs with a telephoto lens. Never feed or follow wild animals. Learn about wildlife so that you know when they are likely to be mating, breeding and protecting their young. At these times, always give animals a wide berth.

## AT YOUR CAMPSITE

From the moment you arrive at your campsite make an effort to minimize your impact on it by carefully selecting where you pitch your tents, do your cooking, store your food and so on. In this way, you will have less cleaning up to do when you leave and the area should look almost the same as when you arrived.

Leave yourself plenty of time to do a thorough site clean-up when leaving. Walk around the area and gather up your trash, especially in the kitchen area. Only burn trash if you are absolutely sure that it will be completely destroyed by the fire. Collect the rest up and store it in large closely sealed plastic 'garbage' bags that will trap any smell and that can be compressed for carting out. It is important to pack your trash our rather than bury it because animals have a keen sense of smell and they will pick up the odour and dig it up. After that they might become frequent visitors to the campsite and that could be dangerous for both campers and animals.

- If you take it in, you must take it out. Leave no trace of your visit behind and if you spot someone else's litter, cart that out as well.
- Light fires if permitted responsibly and don't let them get out of control.
- Don't trespass, don't dig up plants or collect rocks or historical artefacts.
- Leave gates or openings just as you find them – open or closed.
- Don't pollute water supplies – bury human waste in the ground and make sure it is at least 30 m (100 feet) from water courses.
- Observe all warnings and regulations posted by the authorities.
- Respect the peace, solitude and tranquility by keeping noise to a minimum.

# A WORD ON WEATHER FORECASTING

Never head into the countryside without first checking the forecast, and while you are away always keep an eye on what the weather is doing. By constantly monitoring your surroundings, you will usually have enough warning to put warm or wet-weather gear on, and start looking for somewhere safe to ride out a storm. Knowing how to collect water and light a fire in any conditions may well be essential for your survival. Always carry an emergency kit in a waterproof pouch or tin.

If the temperature suddenly drops it could signal the approach of a cold front and that also could mean rain. Learn to recognise cloud formations:

**Cloud formations**

**Cirrus clouds** are very high and in wispy streaks. They usually mean good weather but if they build up in cold climate, coupled with an increase in the wind, a blizzard is likely on its way.

**Cumulus clouds** are lower, white and fluffy and a sign of good weather. However, if they start to pile up on each other, there may be a storm coming.

**Stratus clouds** are low and grey and generally mean rain, while small, wispy scud clouds blown before the wind normally presage bad weather.

Another way of forecasting is to observe nature's own weather forecasters. If there is heavy dew when you wake, the day will probably stay dry. If there is no dew, it will probably rain. Cattle sense approaching rain and will herd together and face away from the direction the rain is coming. Spiders can sense rain and don't spin their webs if it is going to be wet. If it is going to be windy, they will busily spin extra strands to anchor the web, and if it is going to be fine, you will notice spiders' webs everywhere. Many flowers close their petals long before the first drops of rainfall and some trees turn their leaves, showing their much lighter, almost silvery, and this is a sure sign of approaching rain.

If you are in a remote area, it is especially important to be aware of the weather. In the hills, storms often blow up quickly and conditions can deteriorate rapidly. Look out for deer because if a severe storm is coming they break cover and make for lower ground. So, if you observe changes in the weather that could affect your safety, it is a good idea to follow the example of the deer and head down into a valley and be safe.

# NUTRITION

If a normal adult male stayed in bed all day he would need about 1,000 calories just to keep his body functioning, his heart beating regularly, and his temperature up, without losing weight. If an adult female hikes out in the cold, she would need to increase her calorie intake both for energy and to keep warm. If she happened to be backpacking in the hills and carrying a heavy load, her calorie intake needs to soar to 3 to 4,000 calories a day or more. A man would need an even higher calorie intake.

The Sierra Club, the influential environmental organisation, has calculated that you need two and a half times as many calories to gain 300 m (1,000 feet) of elevation as you do to walk at sea level for one hour at 3 kph. For example, an adult, depending on weight, needs between 350 and 500 calories an hour to cover 3 km over rough but relatively flat terrain. To cover the same distance in the same time but ascending to 915 m (3,000 feet) that same adult would need between 850 and 1,250 calories.

The following statistics show the number of calories burned through exercise for adults weighing 60, 70 and 85 kg:

| **Activity (1 hour)** | **60 kg** | **70 kg** | **85 kg** |
|---|---|---|---|
| Backpacking | 413 | 493 | 604 |
| Cycling (16 kph/10 mph) | 236 | 281 | 345 |
| Cycling (off road) | 502 | 598 | 733 |
| Hiking cross country | 354 | 422 | 518 |
| Horseback riding | 236 | 281 | 345 |
| Walking (uphill) | 354 | 422 | 518 |

Knowing what to take with you and why is critical when heading off on the track. Work out what activity and energy requirements your trip will involve to determine the level of calorie intake you will need. If the calories you consume equal calories you burn, you will have enough energy from your food for your trip. You might even put on a little weight as the exercise and activity converts body fat to muscle, which is heavier.

The three basic ingredients of your diet are protein, carbohydrate and fat. In the city if you are leading a sedentary job and eat a normal diet, you want to reduce fat intake because it is easily metabolized into body fat. In the wilderness, you need fat in your diet because if you are walking you are burning lots of calories and you need to convert fat into energy to fuel the body.

If your calorie intake is too low, you will burn body fat and lose weight. This is an inefficient way of providing energy as it takes about 10 per cent more oxygen to release energy from body fat than from carbohydrate, which means there will be less oxygen available to pump through the muscles and you will tire sooner.

Even if you are out walking for just a few hours during the cold months, you will need more energy just to keep warm. In hot weather, your energy requirements may be lower but your liquid requirements increase. Sweating can lead to dehydration and hypo-thermia in the cold, and dehydration and heatstroke in hot weather. It has been estimated that a walker carrying a 16-kg (35-lb) pack in difficult terrain in very hot weather can lose up to 800 ml (1.75 pints) an hour from perspiration, and this is in addition to normal daily water loss of about 1.3 l (2.75 pints) through breathing, sweating and urinating.

It is vital to drink lots of liquids. Water is the most essential nutrient of all, as it is great for getting fluid back into the system, but it doesn't replace essential minerals and electrolytes lost through sustained sweating. You can replenish these by drinking diluted sports-type drinks and plenty of liquids in the forms of soups, stews and tea.

When you are on the track you can push up your intake of carbohydrate and fat because these are readily converted to glycogen, the fuel needed to drive muscles and keep energy levels high. You can also snack to keep the fuel tank topped up so that you don't deplete carbohydrate stored as glycogen in your muscles and liver.

If you choose a high-fat diet you will get more calories from less food and this will reduce your pack weight: 1 tsp of butter (fat) contains 45 calories, more than twice as many as is contained in one teaspoon of sugar (carbohydrate). Protein is calorie-rich but energy is wasted converting it into glycogen. Fat tastes good so we get the pleasure of eating it, and it slows down digestion so there is a more even absorption of body fuel, which makes us feel full. Fats take longer to digest and convert into fuel but they provide a more sustained energy level. However, fat is only metabolised if the body has enough carbohydrates to get the reaction going.

If you need a quick energy fix, consume simple carbohydrates, found in candy and fruit. You can sometimes feel the surge of energy as the sugars get into your system. The

downside is that it isn't sustained, so after the initial high, your energy levels can drop significantly leaving you feeling fatigued.

For maximum energy on the track, therefore, consume fat together with complex carbohydrates and protein. You want food that not only provides energy but that is healthy and above all, tastes good. The body takes longer to break down complex carbohydrates, like vegetables, nuts, seeds and grain, so they are released slower into the system and their effect is longer lasting. Protein – meat, fish, cheese and so on – is essential for general well being. It helps build muscles and repair damaged tissue.

# FOOD PLANNING

Careful planning will ensure that you not only have enough food but that it is the right food. You will need to know how many people will be travelling with you, how long you will be away, what terrain you will be covering and what weather you are likely to encounter. Once you know that, you can plan the menus, and amend or adjust to take into account likely weather changes and cooking conditions.

Another consideration is climate. Fresh produce will perish sooner in very hot weather and you will need to drink a lot more water. Meals take longer to prepare in extreme cold or at altitude, so if you are on the track during very cold weather carry more fuel and plan a high-fat, high-carb diet. Pack foods with a low water content (i.e., crackers instead of bread) as they are less likely to freeze. Setting up camp in extreme wet involves keeping your gear as dry as possible before you can concentrate on cooking. This is when a great meal cooked under tough conditions will boost morale and take minds off the weather. If it's all too much, then the snacks and comfort foods really come into their own.

## FOOD CHOICES

**Fresh foods** always taste best but there is a limit to how much you can take if you are planning to be away for several days. We once went on a canoeing trip in Algonquin Provincial Park in northern Ontario and ate fresh meat for a week. Even though it was

## Trailside tips:

- If your trip is over several weeks and you plan to visit some towns, pack special provisions that can be mailed to yourself at a point on your itinerary. This will top up supplies less readily available, or refresh your meal ideas.
- Save fuel by undercooking foods slightly and letting them sit for a few moments, covered, to finish cooking. This works best with vegetables.
- It's always a nice idea to pack a 'surprise' treat to pull out of the pack when your party least expects it, and perhaps most needs it. Liquorice, peanuts and raisins or sweets – high energy, high morale!

June, the water was so cold we suspended our meat supplies in waterproof bags under the canoe. The older the meat became the longer we cooked it just to be on the safe side, but we are both still around to tell the tale!

Many breads, biscuits and crackers can be safely kept for several days. Hard cheeses last a long time, as do rice and pasta. Peanut butter lasts well and is best re-packed to reduce bulk and weight. Take measured portions of powdered mixes in plastic bags ready for making breads and pancakes. Clarified butter is a better choice than margarine, and carob rather than chocolate, when in hot climates, as these both have higher melting points.

**Dehydrated foods** are light and quick to prepare. Manufactured dehydrated meals are nutritionally balanced and readily available, and generally delicious. Simply add water, bring to the boil, simmer for a few minutes and eat. We always pack some manufactured dehydrated meals because apart from providing 'fast' food when you are really tired or up against the elements, they also make excellent emergency rations. Most dehydrated meals have a long shelf life so that if you don't use them on one trip, they can be reserved ready for the next.

While there is a place for these products in emergencies, that is not what this book is about. Dehydrated foods that you have prepared yourself can be included in your menu planning. Drying is an ancient form of preserving food by removing the moisture on which bacteria, moulds and yeasts can grow. You can dry fruits, vegetables, mushrooms and meats to reduce bulk, make them lighter to carry and extend their shelf life. Thinly sliced cold meats such as turkey, chicken, beef and ham all dehydrate well and make excellent snacks that do not need reconstituting, or they are ideal to take with you to add to soups, stews and other recipes. It is best to freeze home-produced dehydrated foods if they are not going to be used for some time, but they can be safely stored in airtight bags in a cool place for a few days before you head out.

**Do-it-yourself dehydrating** dehydrating is easy when using either a conventional oven or a commercial dehydrator. A commercial dehydrator usually has several trays with automatic heat and air-flow controls. Unless you plan to do lots of dehydrating, save the expense and use your kitchen oven.

When you use dehydrated produce in a recipe, simply add water and allow time for it to reconstitute. A good rule of thumb is 400 ml water to 1 cup dried produce. Don't add too much water or the produce will go mushy. If it does need more water, you can add it judiciously during the soaking process. Soak overnight. Alternatively mix with water in a tightly sealed plastic bag after lunch and allow it to reconstitute as you walk during the afternoon so that it is ready to eat for dinner. Most produce needs two to three hours to reconstitute. If you are in a hurry you can pour boiling water over dried fruit and vegetables, let stand for a few minutes and then drain. Dried vegetables being added to soups and stews do not need soaking and can be added directly to the dish, which must then be brought to the boil and simmered.

## How to dehydrate

**Cut large items** like apples, peaches, apricots, pears, peppers, courgettes and onions into thick slices. Smaller fruit and vegetables can be dried whole.

**Take a large baking tray** for each shelf in your oven. One tray will hold up to 1 kg (2 lbs) of prepared produce evenly spread out. Make sure there is enough room for air to circulate freely around the food.

**Preheat the oven to 65°C (150°F).** Place the produce on the trays into the oven. This initial heat drives the moisture from the food. When the surface of the food feels dry, reduce the heat to 60°C (140°F). This is the most critical phase because you don't want to dry too fast or the food will taste leathery. This final drying phase can take between five and eight hours. The oven door should be slightly open so that the moisture can escape and if the oven doesn't have a fan, use an electric fan in front of the open oven door to ensure good air circulation.

**Every 30 minutes or so,** rotate the trays and turn the food occasionally to ensure it dries evenly and does not stick.

**To dehydrate an entire meal,** for example, a stew or similar, simply spread the meal evenly on a tray and dry in the oven in the same way.

**Once dried and cool,** the food can be stored in sealable plastic bags and kept in a cool, dark place indefinitely.

✪ This symbol on recipes and listings indicates when ingredients can be dehydrated.

**Herbs and spices** take up so little room that you should always carry a selection to add flavour to meals. Spice up your food with plenty of garlic as well as paprika or cayenne pepper, especially on a cold night. Many herbs have other benefits as well. Basil, for instance, helps suppress nausea and vomiting; ginger is excellent for settling upset stomachs.

**Comfort foods** are an essential part of your camp larder. Few things are as comforting as a chocolate bar when you are wet and feeling weary. Always have a selection to eat as a treat when you are feeling down, or as a reward when you have successfully accomplished a tough part of the route.

**Energy drinks** are generally 6–10 per cent carbohydrate – great for both energy and to support your immune system. However, sports drinks are best consumed before and immediately after exercise and water should be drunk during exercising. This is because sports drinks require more digestion, while water is absorbed faster.

**Food safety** is important especially in hot weather. Even in the wilderness you should practise good hygiene – wash your hands and keep your utensils and pots clean using biodegradable soap. Disposable wipes are useful for quick cleansing. Double-wrap food

## Trailside tips:

- You can easily make your own sports drink. Simply combine 1 cup natural fruit juice with 1 cup water, add a pinch of salt and shake well.
- Hard cheeses last well on a hike, especially those that have a wax coat. Extend the life of Cheddar or other hard cheeses by coating them in paraffin. It's simple: melt the paraffin in a pan and then, with a pastry brush, apply a coat to the outer rind of the cheese. Ensure there are no bubbles in the coating. Allow to dry, then repeat until there is a solid, smooth coat.
- No recipe is sacred and you can always add dried, rehydrated vegetables and meats. Add special treats such as sun-dried tomatoes or dried shitake mushrooms.
- Raisins can be added to a wide range of dishes for sweetness and extra calories.

and don't allow contact that can lead to cross contamination. Keep food in airtight containers and don't open packets until you need them.

**Foraging** Depending on the time of year and any regulations regarding harvesting of plants and animals, you may be able to supplement your diet with berries, fruits and nuts. If you are close to water or the coast, there could be fish and shellfish. One of the pleasures of being in the wild is being able to recognise which plants are safe to eat and which should be left well alone. Many plants have medicinal or therapeutic properties that can be useful along the way. Willow bark can be chewed to reduce inflammation and pain; the juice from aloe can be used to treat sunburn and bites – snap open a spiky leaf and rub the juice on the affected areas; lemon grass rubbed on your skin will keep mosquitoes away. You won't find all plants in all habitats and regions, so it does pay to identify those that you may come across.

**Fuel** If you are able to light wood fires, fuel is not likely to be a problem and so cooking times are less of an issue. If you are relying on a single camping stove, you will probably need to conserve fuel and this will determine what meals you prepare.

**Labeled rations** It may sound unnecessary but it does make life so much easier on the trail if everything is pre-labeled. Gather together each day's rations and pack and label breakfast, lunch and dinner ingredients separately. Put them together in one container marked with the day the food is to be eaten. Repeat these so that you have each day's rations self-contained in its own pack. Then you simply divide the packs up between members of the party so that the weight is reasonably distributed throughout the group. Each member carries his or her own supply of snacks and has one or more complete daily meal rations. This provides for them too if, in an emergency, the group gets separated.

# CHAPTER TWO

# CAMPSIDE KITCHEN

When selecting your overnight or base camp, choose your site carefully so that you will be comfortable and enjoy a good night's sleep.

First off, make sure that you are not trespassing. Then check out the area for signs of animal tracks or droppings. Different regions of the world have varying levels of hazard from wild animals, so take precautions where necessary against critters raiding the camp overnight for food. Set up the kitchen well away from the sleeping tents. Try to avoid positions under dead trees or very tall ones, which are the more likely to get struck by lightning, and never camp in a dry gorge, at the bottom of a valley or next to a stream. It is not only colder here, you may get washed out if it rains heavily. Conversely, don't camp on top of a rise because you will be too exposed.

The best place to pitch your tent is an area just beneath the brow of a hill on the leeward side. Find a spot with low, natural cover so that if it does rain, it will not become too muddy. Ideally, it should be almost flat, with a slight slope for drainage, and sheltered from the prevailing wind. If you do have to camp on a slope, always sleep with your head uphill.

Clear the area of sticks and stones and anything else that might damage your tent and jab you as you try to sleep. With luck you will find the perfect spot that will be exposed to the rising sun in the morning, to dry out your tent and warm you up as you rise and prepare for the day, and tuck into a hearty breakfast.

# SETTING UP CAMP

Unless the weather is bad, it is a good idea to set up your kitchen and cooking area some distance from the sleeping tents. Select a site that is flat and near some trees that will offer some shade, although setting up the kitchen under overhanging branches could mean you have to deal with drips and falling debris should there be a downpour.

## SHADE AND PROTECTION

Shade offers protection from the elements for both your cooking area and your tents and, in the camp kitchen, protects food from the sun and the fire from the wind. If you cannot find natural shade, create your own by building a screen using branches, a tarpaulin or a groundsheet. If there is heavy snow, pile it up to create a windshield. In very hot or wet weather, make a roof over the cooking area for protection from the rain. A makeshift roof should be high enough to allow you to stand up straight and move around beneath it, and allow smoke to escape.

## LIGHTING

A good torch or headlamp is absolutely essential and each member of the party should have one plus a spare set of batteries in a waterproof container. A headlamp is invaluable. It is great for cooking, walking around the campsite at night and reading in bed. Many headlamps have multiple functions, allowing you to concentrate the beam, or in an emergency to activate a pulsating strobe to signal your position.

Camping lanterns powered by paraffin or liquid petroleum provide good campsite lighting. However, they are bulky and you do have to carry the fuel. Battery lanterns are safe to use inside the tent. Candle lanterns can be used inside a tent for reading before you turn in for the night, but always use them with caution – a candle can melt tent fabric in the blink of an eye – and extinguish them before you doze off.

## STORAGE

Keep the entire camp area clean and always ensure you clear away any dropped food in the camp kitchen area to avoid attracting animals and insects. It is a good rule never to store food in or near your tent. Keep all food (and other items like toothpaste and deodorants) in storage containers. When not needed, hang food from a tree branch well off the ground and away from the trunk if possible. If there are no trees, dangle your food containers over an overhang or pile up all your equipment around the food and place rocks, pots and pans on top. If an animal interferes with the pile, the falling pots might just frighten it away. Food can be sealed in plastic bags inside a closed rucksack so that the scent does not attract animals in the area or pesky pests. Keep dried foods in waterproof containers – you don't want them getting wet accidentally or prematurely – and stand the containers on rocks and cover with a tarpaulin for added protection.

Keep perishable foods in a cooler, if you take one, or if you are near cold, fast-running water, you can use this as a natural cooler for a day or two. Place the food inside a watertight bag. Attach one end of a length of rope securely to the bag and submerge it. Secure the other end of the rope to a tree trunk or around a large rock. If the water is not too deep you can push some sticks into the river or lake bed around the bag so that if the rope comes undone, the bag will not wash away. In very high temperatures, ensure you check carefully that food has not gone off.

Take as much trouble to gather up your rubbish. Store it in large, tightly sealed plastic bags that will trap any smell and that can be compressed for carting out.

# COOKING METHODS

Nothing beats cooking a meal over an open fire. The food seems to taste better, you can utilise the embers (not the flames) to bake potatoes and root vegetables, and you can sit around it and enjoy the conviviality of each other's company. However, in many of the world's wild regions it is prohibited to light campfires, and many areas will post fire hazard ratings on approach roads or in the offices of parks.

Nonetheless, where it is safe and legal there are two options for an open fire: a teepee-type fire where pots are suspended over the heat, or a "T" fire, where the fire is lit in the top cross part of the T and its embers are raked into the bottom part, and used for cooking. The hottest embers are in one half of the cooking area and the less hot embers in the other half, giving one area in which to cook fast, and another in which to simmer or keep food warm in its pan.

**Damper or stone fires** are best built in a pit. Wood is used for fuel and two or three large, flat stones are positioned in the centre of the fire to become hot. It is absolutely essential the stones be of non-porous rock, otherwise they may shatter when hot and send fragments in all directions. Once the fire is burning well it can be collapsed so that it rings the stones, and the pots are then placed on the hot stones for cooking. One or two large stones can be positioned on the perimeter of the fire where they will not be so hot, and be used to keep cooked food warm. The stones can also provide the base for a grill for even more stability for pots or a Dutch oven, or for use as a griddle.

## BACKPACKER STOVES

When using a camping stove, create a flat base on which to stand it, and position it to benefit from the windscreen to ensure the stove stays alight and the flames are able to heat the pot. Keep spare fuel away from the lit stove.

If it is raining or snowing hard when you erect the tent, pitch it so that the opening is protected as much as possible from the elements. Pack up stones or logs in a semi-circular wall to create a windbreak. Use your rucksack to create additional protection against wind and rain. You can then sit in the tent and cook in the opening, ensuring that there is a lot of ventilation. Have a container of water close by, in case the stove flares up or the pot spills and burns you. By the time you have finished eating your meal you will not only feel so much better, the weather may have improved.

Stoves are more convenient to cook with than open fires: they can be set up in most situations, be instantly aflame, the temperature is controllable and they have minimal impact on the environment. Their downside is that the fuel they require must be carried.

Small stoves are safest when placed on a firm, even surface such as a large flat rock. As a general rule never cook on a stove inside a tent because of the danger of a flare-up or build-up of carbon monoxide. In extreme conditions, it may be necessary to cook in the entrance of a tent but only if there is adequate ventilation.

There are many types of stove available from the lightweight, compact single burners to double burners and large family camping models that need to be ferried by vehicle.

A number of different fuels are used. Petrol and paraffin stoves use liquid fuel which vaporises on its way to the burner. Here, it combines with oxygen in the air and is ignited. The fuel is contained in a flask that connects to the stove via flexible tube. The fuel is commonly available, but it does smell and can contaminate food if it leaks. These stoves tend to perform better than other types in extremely cold weather or at high altitude.

**Liquid petroleum (LP)** stoves run on propane, butane, or a mixture of the two and are by far the most popular worldwide. They are lightweight, convenient and effective. You can buy pressurised canisters of different capacities depending on the length of your trip or the number you are cooking for. Full canisters are not heavy but all have to be carried in (and out). A single burner stove screws into the canister and a valve turns the gas on and off, and some models have automatic ignition. The flame can be regulated, and therefore the temperature, by how far the valve is open. If it is windy, the flames are blown laterally and therefore much of the heat is wasted. At altitude, it takes much longer to heat anything because of the difference in pressure, and for this reason LP stoves are less effective than liquid fuel (petrol or paraffin) stoves in very cold weather.

**The Trangia** ™ stove is original in that its design principle developed specially for cooking in high winds and severe cold. The Swedish-made stove is lightweight, reliable, and very compact. The smaller series is ideal for solo or two backpackers, while the larger one can easily cope with a camping group of three to four. The stove packs inside an aluminium two-pan set, complete with windshield, lids and burner and a strap to hold it all together. Trangia stoves burn methylated spirit, which is cheap, readily available and can be carried in Trangia's purpose-made lightweight plastic fuel bottles. The stove can also run on bottled gas with a gas burner accessory. Its great advantage is that there are no moving parts, pipes or valves to break. Simply pour the fuel into the burner and ignite.

**White gas** (Naphtha/Coleman fuel) stoves are common in North America, but the fuel is not always readily available elsewhere, so many white gas stoves can be converted to burn other fuels. Multi-fuel stoves cost more than single-fuel models but if you are planning to visit several destinations, the added flexibility is worth the extra cost.

## DUTCH OVENS

Dutch ovens work wonderfully on an open fire, on the grill or even on the stove back home. They are cooking pots made from cast-iron or aluminium, and are available in varying sizes from a small 10 cm to the huge 60 cm model. A 25–30 cm Dutch oven is the best for group cooking. While classified as cooking pots they are much more versatile than most pots. The internal base can be used as a griddle and the inside space as a large pot or casserole. You can pile embers on top as well and use the pot as an oven by applying heat to the top and bottom.

## Dutch oven techniques

**Baking:** You need more heat from the top, so pile embers on the lid.

**Boiling:** All the heat needs to come from underneath.

**Frying:** You need heat from below only and cook directly on the bottom of the oven.

**Griddle:** Use the lid upside down as a griddle or skillet for great pancakes.

**Roasting:** For best results there should be equal heat from top and bottom.

**Stewing:** Most of the heat should come from below the oven with just a few embers on the lid.

Cast-iron ovens are very heavy and really only suitable for a static camp kitchen or if you come in by vehicle. Aluminium ovens are lighter and can be carried in a backpack. While they take up a lot of room, you can pack items inside to utilise the space fully. Aluminium Dutch ovens heat up more quickly and reflect heat which can lead to temperature fluctuations while cooking. Choose an oven that has three legs as the base must never be allowed to sit directly on hot embers. The legs enable it to straddle the embers so that there is no direct contact with them. Select one that has a lid with a ridge around the rim so that you can put hot embers on top without them sliding off.

It is advisable to prepare a new Dutch oven by putting it in a pre-heated oven three times. The first time drives out any trapped water. Before warming the second and third time, completely cover the Dutch oven inside and out with a thin film of vegetable oil so that when baked, it forms a protective layer.

## Trailside tips:

- Choose a Dutch oven that has a heavy-duty handle on the base and the lid and has three legs. The legs allow you to stand the oven in the embers without resting on them. This allows air to circulate under the oven and fan the flames.
- Dutch ovens get very hot! Thick gloves are essential and a pot gripper is useful for removing the lid. When full, slide a stout pole through the handle so that two people can lift the oven from the fire.

# ESSENTIAL EQUIPMENT

As far as possible, research the conditions you are likely to experience along the way. When hiking a long-distance path, consider whether there will be adequate water supplies along the way or whether you have to carry in all your water? If you plan to set up camp and then travel out each day, what facilities are available? There may be picnic benches and a barbecue pit, for instance, and you will not therefore need to take all of your own cooking equipment. What cooking methods are you undertaking? How many in your party? How is that going to affect what utensils you require? Each of these aspects will be your main considerations to ensure that you are well enough equipped.

## POTS

Nesting cookware sets are like Russian dolls: they are comprised of a large pot containing three or four smaller pots. The lids of the pots are multi-functional and can be used as bowls, frying pans and even plates. Instead of pot and lid handles, one or two pot grippers are incorporated for removing lids or hot pots from the stove, and this makes the sets compact when packed. Typically these sets are made from aluminium. A variety of sizes and numbers of pots are available to suit different-size parties.

| Solo campers require a set comprising: | Two people require a set that provides: | For four or more people, you need: |
|---|---|---|
| **1** 1.1-litre pot | **1** 1.6-litre pot | **1** 1.6-litre pot |
| **1** 1.6-litre pot | **1** 2.7-litre pot | **1** 2.2-litre pot |
| **2** lids become 2 frying pans, bowls or plates | **2** lids become 2 frying pans, bowls or plates | **1** 2.7-litre pot with lid |
| **1** pot gripper | **1** pot gripper | **1** 19-cm frying pan |
| | | **2** lids become frying pan, bowls or plates |
| | | **2** pot grippers |

## UTENSILS

You will need plates, mugs, bowls, knives, forks and spoons and basic cooking utensils, such as a sharp knife to cut bread, fish, vegetables, even wood; a spatula; larger spoons for serving and mixing; pot gripper or holder (if not included in the pot kit). Select pot kits of the best quality you can afford – good cookware is a pleasure to use, especially under camp conditions. Ensure all utensils are light and durable and above all, choose those you are comfortable using.

### Trailside tips:

- Paint pot grippers a bright colour or bind with reflective tape so that you can spot them easily.
- Film canisters make great containers to hold spices and small portions of jam and butter.

## OTHER ESSENTIALS

**Aluminium foil** has countless uses on the campsite. Use it to sachet food that can be dropped in to the hot embers to cook. Make a frame from wooden twigs and branches and completely cover it with foil to make a griddle. Use foil as a heat reflector or to line the base of a Dutch oven to make it easier to clean. Use it to wrap left-over food. In an emergency you can even wrap yourself in foil to keep warm or signal for help.

**Plastic bags** Always carry several plastic bags of different sizes. Heavy-duty freezer bags and zip-seal bags are best. They weigh almost nothing, yet are worth their weight in gold. Use them to mix food ingredients, marinate dishes, collect water, to pack food, rubbish and a host of other things. You can even crack eggs into a plastic bag, add salt and pepper, and then suspend it in the coffee pot. As the coffee begins to heat up, so it cooks the eggs.

Pack ingredients for breakfasts, lunches and dinners separately into clearly labelled plastic bags, and then make up one large bag for each day away. The large bag contains all the food needed for that day, and means you don't have to disturb another day's rations until required.

**Water carriers** Choose from collapsible plastic water containers with screw-tops, plastic and fabric collapsible buckets, and any number of water bottles of different shapes and sizes. You must take a water carrier, but cooking pots and even hats can be used to collect small quantities of water.

Collected natural water must be sterilised. Even water from high altitude may be contaminated so don't take chances. Either use purification tablets or bring water to the boil, and boil for at least a further minute. Boiling for longer than this is not necessary and wastes fuel, and if you are using the water for cooking, the normal cooking process should be enough to kill any bugs. Carry a personal water bottle and replenish it whenever you get the opportunity, adding purification tablets if necessary.

**Matches** Buy several boxes of windproof, waterproof matches and make sure each member of the party has a box or two. Wrap the boxes in plastic bags for added waterproof protection. Cigarette lighters that are designed to ignite in windy weather are also useful.

**Emergency kit** Your kit should be contained in a tin and include the following: waterproof matches and/or a flint and steel for lighting fires; a couple of tea and coffee bags; chocolate; razor blades; mini torch; candle; water purification tablets; safety pins; needle and thread (for repairs, fishing or sutures); tweezers; antiseptic; fish hooks; whistle, and a second compass. Check your kit before each trip – hopefully it will be only be the chocolate that needs replacing.

## CLEARING AND DISPOSAL

**Water disposal** If there is running water nearby, gather it into a container to wash dirty dishes, using biodegradable soap or better, by scrubbing with a handful of grass and sand. Never leave dirty dishes out because they will attract unwelcome guests. Dispose of the dirty dish water away from a lake or stream.

**Litter disposal and campsite clearing** Always clean up the site to leave no trace you were ever there. Pick up any litter and pack in bags for carrying out. Clear up any spillages. Try to return the site to the condition it was in when you arrived. Pack up all your camping equipment and possessions.

**Fire safety** Dismantle any fire walls and scatter fire ash and any unburned wood over as wide an area as possible. Then check thoroughly around the campsite to make sure any fire ash is totally extinguished and that you have not left anything behind. Do a final walk round to double check you have everything.

# NATURE'S LARDER

Whether you are running low on food because you've gobbled up your supplies more quickly than anticipated, or you simply want a change of fare, there is no reason to go hungry on a hike, at least in some types of terrain. In lake country or beside the ocean, there may be fish and crustaceans available. Indeed, there is nothing more delicious than fresh-caught fish cooked on an open fire.

## FISH FOR SUPPER

Whenever you go off hiking, always carry a couple of fish hooks and some line in your emergency kit (see page 35). Cut a suitable branch for a rod, attach the line and hook and see what you can land. You will need to bait the hook, so dig down for a juicy worm, check foliage for insect larvae or peel back some tree bark to find maggots or grubs. If wood branches are difficult to find, fish, simply using a baited line secured on the riverbank or lake edge with the baited end trailing in the water. Set up a number of lines and check them frequently to see if you have a bite.

To prepare a fish for cooking, place it on its side, slice open down the belly, from the gills to the tail, and scrape out all internal organs. Wash the internal cavity thoroughly and cut off the fins. Then cut into the spine until you touch the backbone and slice the blade down either side of the backbone, filleting the meat away from the bones.

Cook your catch by skewering it onto a stick and roasting it over the fire – as it cooks it can fall apart into the fire so this method is only effective if your fish is a sizeable catch. Alternatively, wrap it in foil and bury the package in the embers of the fire or poach it in

**AVOID FOODS THAT**

- You don't recognise or cannot identify from field guides.
- Smell bad or are decaying.
- Have a three-leafed growth pattern.
- Are overripe or contain a milky sap.
- Contain seeds in a pod.
- Smell of almonds – they may contain cyanide compounds.
- Are growing in, or close to, polluted water.

water in a pot or skillet. The latter method has the benefit that you can use the liquid as a sauce, adding whatever natural ingredients you can find, such as nuts, leaves, wild garlic or anything else that provides a nutritious, if unusual, meal!

## FORAGING FOR SURVIVAL

The most innocent trip can turn into a disaster. What happens if you get separated from the rest of your group? And they have all the food? Hopefully, you and they will back-track. But if you don't know the way back, you will have to fall back on your survival skills to make it home safely. How you forage for food will depend on what terrain you are in and at what time of the year it is. Water is the most critical requirement. An adult can live for three or four weeks without food but will perish after just a few days without water. If you have to forage for food, put aside squeamishness because you won't have the luxury to decide what you would rather not put in your mouth! Many insects and grubs are edible, raw or cooked, and packed with protein. Young shoots, berries, fruits and roots of many plants are not only edible but tasty too. While some fungi are delicious, you must positively identify the species. Many fungi are not only disgusting to taste, but more importantly utterly deadly. Only eat fungi that you have confidently identified as safe. Always use good field guides to the region you are walking, to identify animals and plants you are likely to encounter. Obviously, survival skills required when alone in the wilderness areas of North America will be very different to those required in the Australian Outback or Scottish mountains. Inform yourself fully before you set out.

# FINDING NATURAL WATER

You can't survive for long without water and this is especially true if you are trekking through an arid wilderness. Water constituents about 60 percent of total body weight and every system and organ in your body depends on it. The average adult sedentary male loses up to 2¾ pints (1.3l) of water every day. Put on a heavy pack and start hiking over difficult terrain and you really start to sweat. A walker carrying a heavy pack in these conditions can lose up to 1¾ pints (800ml) an hour from perspiration. That is why you must drink lots of water and other liquids to replenish lost fluids, minerals and electrolytes. If you are running low on water, avoid eating fatty foods because they require more body water to break them down.

The easiest way to locate a water source is to look at a map for a nearby stream, lake or geological feature where water might collect. There are certain indicators to look out for depending in your terrain. Before setting out to find water, however, make sure you have something to collect it in. A collapsible plastic bucket or plastic bottle is best for larger quantities, or a spoon or straw will allow you to scoop up tiny quantities.

**Mountains** You are more likely to find water at the foot of a gentle slope than a steep slope. Follow valleys down looking for springs, pools or streams. If the vegetation suddenly gets very lush, look for water nearby.

**Countryside** A row of alder or willows in the distance or a line of grass taller than the rest usually indicates a stream or water source. During the spring, many trees, including maple and birch, contain water with a high sugar content. In an emergency, gouge a hole in the trunk (use a knife or stone) and then use a piece of bark to funnel the escaping liquid into a container. In the early morning, mop up dew and squeeze into your mouth or a container. Gather it before dawn because it will evaporate quickly as the sun rises. Animals know where to get water, so follow tracks.

**Desert** If you see birds or green vegetation, there is usually water nearby. Many desert plants, especially cacti, contain water. Dew often forms on rocks around dawn, and you may also find traces of water dripping from the roofs of  caves or running down large cracks in a rock. Dry stream beds are a good place to look. Dig down and you may find damp earth, dig further and you may find water.

**Tropics** Frequent downpours and areas of standing water mean that water is not usually a problem. Many trees, plants and vines contain water like the banana. Chop the banana plant down to leave a stem about 3 feet (1 meter) above the ground. Scoop out the center of the stem and it will start to fill up with water from the roots. It will continue to provide water for two or three days so cover the stem to protect the water from insects and birds.

**Glaciers and snow-laden areas** There is no problem getting water in areas where there is ice and snow. The problem is that it takes energy to convert either into drinkable water. Melt ice rather than snow because it will yield more water. If you have to melt snow, melt a little at a time and then add more. Break ice on streams and lakes to find running water. You should boil melted ice well to purify it.

## PURIFYING WATER

Even when water looks clean enough to drink there may be bugs lurking so it does pay to take basic precautions. To cleanse any natural water you collect, bring it to the boil and boil it for a full minute. Alternatively, add purification tablets according to the instructions on the packaging.

A third method is to use a water filter. The Katadyn Hiker Water Filter weighs only 312 g and can yield up to 755 litres of potable water before the filter needs replacing. You simply place one end of a plastic tube in the water and then pump it through the filter into your container. If scooping up larger amounts of water, let it stand for between 30 minutes and an hour to allow silt and sand to settle in the bottom of the container and then filter into another container. Don't disturb the silt.

Filter straws, just a little larger than a conventional straw, can be used to suck up small pools of water. Once the filter is full, no more water can be produced. This means that you can safely use it to get potable water from even the foulest-looking sources.

## Trailside tips:

- It is important not to contaminate natural water sources with dirty soapy water from your dishes, washing or toilet. Washing and the disposal of human waste must be done carefully so the environment is not polluted and fish and aquatic life are not injured.

# CHAPTER THREE

## GET SET . . . PACK

The average holiday-maker returns from a trip having worn only two thirds of the clothes taken away. The rest were, in every sense, excess baggage. When you are packing in readiness for backpacking over several days, you must pack only what you truly need because a) you are going to have to carry it all the way throughout the day, there and back; and b) space is limited. Experienced backpackers know exactly what they need and will assemble the most efficient and the lightest kit they can.

We have friends who drill holes in the handles of their toothbrush to reduce weight. They take paperback books and each day use the pages they have read to light the fire. You don't need to go to these extremes to put together a pack that is light yet still contains everything you will need to have both a comfortable and enjoyable trip. Just think very carefully about how much you will really use each item that you are considering putting into your pack. You may consider leaving heavy items, particularly bulky cookware, in the car so you have them on hand when you need them but won't have to haul them around when you don't.

# PACK LIGHT

Thanks to the wonder of modern technology that is applied to lightweight equipment, a pack containing all your needs for a four-day trip weighs today about half as much as it might have done 20 years ago. A pack containing tent, sleeping bag and mat, stove, fuel, water, food, clothes, wet-weather gear and other essentials need weigh no more than 13.5 kg. With the lightest gear available you can readily cut down on this by a few kilograms even further.

A three-season sleeping bag weighing 1 kg, when used in conjunction with an all-weather bivouac bag, will provide a 1.3-kg combo that will keep you alive in the most extreme conditions – and you won't even need a tent.

If you want the luxury of a tent, you can get a three-season, two-person tent weighing around 1.8 kg. Add to that a lightweight stove, fuel, a set of cooking pots, a collapsible plastic bucket, torch, first-aid and emergency kit, and you have all the main camping needs weighing at little more than 4.5 kg. All of this has to go into your pack, together with wet-weather gear, clothing, food and whatever else you want to take on with you.

**Stuff sacs** come in different sizes and it is useful to have several, in different colours, for wet-weather gear, clothing, sleeping bag and so on. Stuff sacs are effective because once a sac is filled, and all the air is pressed out, it becomes as compressed as possible, and you can then secure it so that the sac cannot expand. Even a bulky sleeping bag can be compressed to a quarter of its size in this way. It will not reduce the weight, but it does mean you can carry more and everything is kept orderly, which makes life a lot easier on a hike of several days.

### HOW MUCH FOOD TO TAKE?

If you are on the hike for just one day or a weekend, you can follow the sort of diet that you would at home. The extra energy expended will burn off some surplus (unless you are super fit). However, if you are planning to be out for several days or even weeks, you will need to adjust your diet accordingly because you will want a more energy-efficient calorie-rich diet.

There are several ways to calculate how much food you will need – calories required per person, weight of food per person and so on – but the easiest method is to create a meal plan.

We work out what makes a nutritious menu that provides three hearty meals a day; we then add enough snacks and treats to ensure that we get the right mix of nutrients and the required number of calories. Several days before you set out write out your menu plan. Here's an example:

| Sample meal plan | |
|---|---|
| **Day 1** | Bacon and eggs on a bagel • Swedish apple soup • Vegetarian chilli • Pineapple sundae • Trail mix/energy bars |
| **Day 2** | Banana pancakes • Pitta pizza • Goulash • Coconut surprise • Trail mix/energy bars |
| **Day 3** | Fruit treat • Summa' soup • Lemon couscous • Chocolate fondue • Trail mix/energy bars |
| **Day 4** | Breakfast casserole • No-pot stew • Pasta Alfredo • Berries galore • Trail mix/energy bars |

Menu planning helps focus on the perishable foods and identifies meal-by-meal what you need to prepare in advance, and what ingredients you need to have as staples at camp .

Draw up a list of all the ingredients required. Quantities will, of course, be determined by how many people are in the group. Check off any you already have in the cupboard, but do not accidentally omit them at packing.

### LABELLING THE FOOD

When you are ready to pack, lay out all the food items required. Pack the ingredients for each meal into plastic 'meal bags'. For example, a breakfast bag may contain just two or three ingredient bags. A dinner bag may contain up to five ingredient bags. Then pack them all into a 'day bag', which contains all the rations needed for one day's meals. 'Day bags' can be distributed between members of the group. For example, if there are four people out for four days, they each carry one day's bag. Pack 'kitchen bags' of herbs, sauces, seasonings, and so on. Trail mixes and energy bars can be packed separately so that each member carries their own trail mix ration for the trip.

Colour-code meal bags. For example, green labels for breakfast, red for lunch and blue for dinner. Write on each meal bag label what it contains and slip each day's menu plan into its respective day bag. If you are trying a new recipe, pack the instructions as well!

## BACKPACKERS' PROVISIONS

**Foods that keep well on a hike and form the basis for many campside recipes include:**

### Pantry staples

- Coffee and tea bags (or ground coffee)
- Cocoa/hot chocolate drinks
- Sugar/sweetener
- Seasoning, spices and herbs
- Noodles, pasta, rice
- Powdered eggs and milk
- Margarine (or clarified butter) and vegetable oil
- Instant mash potatoes
- Porridge oats/home-made cereal mixes (with added nuts, dried fruit and dried milk)
- Parmesan (grated)
- Stock cubes/extracts
- Peanut butter
- Marshmallows
- Sauces (packets, dehydrated and preferably home-made)
- Dehydrated fruit, vegetables and meats
- Dried beans, pulses and lentils
- Home-made dehydrated soups, stews and casseroles
- Cake mixes
- Flour

### No-cook instants

- Cheese (hard)
- Potato crisps
- Energy and cereal bars
- Fruit slices (dehydrated)
- Dried meats such as salami, pepperoni
- Nuts
- Trail mixes

### Breads and crackers

- Pitta bread (lasts well and packs tightly)
- Bagels (can be toasted if they start to get stale)
- Dry crackers and crisp-breads (to eat with cheese or soup)
- Bake fresh bread every other day (the ingredients weigh less to carry in than the finished product)

### Luxuries

- Chocolate chips (chocolate chip pancakes for breakfast!)
- Chocolate bars
- Cans of pâté and/or caviar
- (And your heart's desires – provided you are willing to carry it!)

### Essential backpack items

- Tent and sleeping gear
- Stove and fuel (separate from food)
- Food
- Utensils
- First-aid kit including tweezers
- Compass
- Emergency kit
- Flashlight
- ID (personal identification)
- Knife – multi-blade (sharp blade, scissors, corkscrew, mini saw, can opener)
- Map
- Matches
- Clothing
- Sandals or trainers (to slip into when the boots come off)
- Socks and sock liners
- Hat
- Sewing kit (for basic repairs, emergency sutures)
- Wet-weather gear
- Water bottle

### Additional items for longer trips

- Fire lighter or flint and steel
- Headlamp or lantern
- Extra batteries for torch
- Washing kit, towel and other personal requirements
- Toilet paper
- Emergency blanket or lightweight tarpaulin
- Nylon rope – 10 m (30 feet)
- Small roll of duct tape
- Small trowel or very lightweight folding shovel (for digging a latrine)
- Water purification tablets/ filter
- Aluminium foil
- MORE FOOD!

### Seasonal requirements

- Gloves
- Insect repellant
- Lip balm
- Sunglasses
- Sunscreen
- Pack cover (a waterproof that slips over your pack to protect it from the rain)
- Small hatchet/folding saw (for chopping firewood)
- Weather radio (lightweight and tuned to receive the forecast for the area)

### Optional items, depending on your interests

- Binoculars (compact)
- Camera (spare batteries/ cards and/or film)
- Playing cards
- Field guides
- Fishing line and hooks
- Wet wipes
- Journey log and pen
- Paperback/magazines (excellent tinder when lighting fires)

## CAMPSITE COMFORTS – IF CONVEYED BY VEHICLE

When you are not carrying everything on your back, but setting up a base campsite, the following items go beyond the basic essentials, but will give camp life that extra degree of gastronomy and comfort:

### Kitchen items

| | | |
|---|---|---|
| Coffee pot | Dishcloths | Paper towels |
| Cooler | Griddle | Plastic wrap |
| Corkscrew | Grill and charcoal | Skillet |
| Cutting board | Measuring cup | Spatulas and spoons |
| Dishwashing bowl | Mixing bowls | Water jugs |

### Overnight comforts

| | | |
|---|---|---|
| Air mattresses (and pump) | Camp chairs and table | Pillows |
| Axe | Canopy | Portable chemical toilet |
| Broom (small) | Fire extinguisher | Shower (solar showers are fun if you have water!) |
| Camp beds | Mallet | |

## Trailside tips:

- If you are heading out on a four-day trip, carry an extra bag containing two main meals, mostly of dehydrated foods. If you are delayed for any reason, you have some back-up food. If it's not needed, you can eat it up back at home.
- Every time you close up a bag, squeeze as much air out as possible, so that it takes up less room.
- Don't take foods that will spoil quickly unless you plan to eat them in the first day or two. Avoid soft cheeses, mayonnaise, butter, fresh eggs and fresh milk.
- Always repack the contents of cans into plastic bags.
- As each day's rations are consumed, the empty bags and any rubbish can be transferred to a 'rubbish bag' that comes home with you.

# SAMPLE MENUS AND PACK LISTS

## One-day hike

• **Trail bread** (p. 116) – French bread, pâté and a selection of hard and soft cheese (cheddar and brie). Prepared, sliced fruit. Eat separately or mix in a pot of yoghurt • **Pitta pizza** (p. 81) • **Trail muesli** (p. 52) Split the mix into two packets – one for morning and one after lunch • Snacks (p. 53–58)

## Packing checklist for one person on a one-day hike

Water
4 tea or coffee bags
Soup for lunch

2 bread rolls
110 g cheddar cheese
Slices of salami

Apple
Trail mix
Energy bar/chocolate bar

## Weekend (two-day) hike

**Day 1** Crusty bread with • **Black bean spread** (p. 84), spread on **crispbread** or **bread** (p. 116) • **Vegetarian chilli** (p. 132), prepared ahead to serve with rice • **Banana boats** (p. 133)

**Day 2** • **Bacon and eggs on a bagel** (p. 71) • **Swedish apple soup** (p. 79) • **Trail mix** and **energy bars** (p. 52–58)

## Packing checklist for two people on a two-day hike

**Staples:**
Water
8 tea or coffee bags
Margarine (in a tube)
Powdered milk
Sugar/sweeteners
Salt and pepper
Cookies (as desired)

**Breakfast:**
4 large pre-cooked rashers bacon
4 eggs or egg powder equivalent
2 bagels

**Lunches:**
Black bean spread (p. 84)
Swedish apple soup (p. 79)
Loaf of crusty bread

**Dinners:**
Vegetarian chilli (p. 132)
200 g rice
2 bananas
4 marshmallows
4 tbsp chocolate chips

**Trail mix/snacks:**
Trail muesli (p. 52)
4 energy bars (pp. 52–58)

| Four-day hike | |
|---|---|
| **Day 1** | • **No-pot stew** (p. 88) • **Lentil chilli** (p. 94) • **Fruit grill** (p. 131) |
| **Day 2** | • **Fruit treat** (p. 66) • **Apple and turkey stir-fry** (p. 89) • **Lemon couscous with chicken** (p. 101) • **Mint chocolate pots** (p. 137) |
| **Day 3** | • **French toast** (p. 72) • **Bacon and Cheddar spread** on crackers (p. 85) • **Banana bread** (p. 122) • **Goulash** (p. 130) • **Pineapple sundae** (p. 127) |
| **Day 4** | • **Banana pancakes** (p. 67) • **Summa' soup** (p. 80) |

**Packing checklist for four people on a four-day hike**

**Staples:**
Water
64 coffee or tea bags
Drum of powdered milk
Sugar or sweeteners
Salt and pepper
Butter or margarine
Vegetable oil
Dried herbs
Cookies

**Breakfasts:**
Fruit treat (p. 66)
8 thick slices bread
6 eggs or egg powder
Vanilla extract
230 g flour
1 tsp baking powder
1 banana

**Lunches:**
2 medium potatoes ✪
3 onions ✪
6 carrots ✪
1 green pepper ✪
4 cloves garlic
Soy sauce
Worcestershire sauce
Cornflour
150 ml apple juice
450 g turkey breast ✪
350 g mange tout/snowpeas ✪
800 g rice
4 stock cubes
150 g dried vegetables
5 rashers bacon
100 g grated cheddar cheese
Salad dressing
Crackers

**Dinners and desserts:**
2 cloves garlic
2 onions ✪
220 g dried lentils
230 g bulghur wheat
3 potatoes ✪
8 stock cubes
1 can chopped tomatoes
Chilli powder
Ground cumin
450 g diced chicken ✪
1 lemon
75 g couscous
Dried herbs
1 lb/450 g ground beef ✪
1 green pepper ✪
2 sticks celery ✪
1 tbsp paprika
100 ml soured cream
175 g noodles
1 kg assorted fruit ✪
15 marshmallows
425 ml chocolate chips
300 ml milk
1 egg
75 g cocoa
50 g flour
1 pineapple
2 oranges
1 banana
225 g strawberries
2 tbsp crystallised ginger
500 ml natural yoghurt

**Snacks:**
25 energy bars
16 x 225-g bags trail muesli (p. 52)

# Trail mixes, boosters & drinks

Snacks are essential supplies on the long-distance path to keep energy levels high, especially if you are walking over rough terrain and carrying a heavy pack. Trail mixes containing nuts, raisins and dried fruits provide a quick energy boost. Energy bars are also important both as carb-loaders and morale boosters.

Drinks are equally crucial to keep the body well hydrated and refuelled with nutrients. If it is chilly, they provide warmth and there is no better feeling than sitting around a campfire under the stars, having enjoyed a great dinner, with a warm drink in your hand.

# Trail muesli

Enjoy this muesli for breakfast or nibble it along the track. Like all trail mixes, you can add your favourite ingredients to make it even more appetising. Makes enough for breakfast for two people plus enough leftovers to supply trail mix for two people for two days.

Makes **8** portions Prep. time: **10** mins Cooking time: **25** mins

| | |
|---|---|
| **8 tbsp/120 g** | **margarine** |
| **1/2 cup/80 g** | **brown sugar** |
| **1 tbsp** | **cinnamon** |
| **4 cups/360 g** | **porridge oats** |
| **2 cups/100 g** | **crushed wheat** |
| **1 cup/100 g** | **wheat germ** |
| **1/2 cup/60 g** | **sesame seeds** |
| **1 cup/150 g** | **mixed raisins and banana slices** |

### At home:

Preheat the oven to 230ºC/450ºF. In a pan over a medium heat, melt the margarine and brown sugar and bring to the boil, stirring continuously. Remove from the heat and stir in the cinnamon. Add the remaining ingredients except the raisins and banana slices, and stir until everything is well combined.

Empty out the mixture on to a 35 x 25-cm baking sheet and spread evenly. Bake in the oven for about 25 minutes.

Remove from the oven and allow to cool on the sheet. Mix in the raisins and banana slices and bag as required.

# Quick energy bar

This is another tasty treat for hikers that will give a fast energy burst if you are feeling weary and still have a few miles to go before stopping for the night. It also freezes well.

Makes 18 bars  Prep. time: 10 mins  Cooking time: 20 mins

| | |
|---|---|
| **4 tbsp** | **margarine** |
| **1 cup/90 g** | **crushed plain digestive biscuits** |
| **1 cup/75 g** | **shredded coconut** |
| **2 cups/450 g** | **chocolate chips** |
| **425-g** | **can condensed milk** |
| **1 cup/150 g** | **chopped walnuts** |
| **3/4 cup/65 g** | **porridge oats** |

## At home:

Preheat the oven to 180ºC/350ºF. Place the margarine on a 35 x 25-cm baking sheet and melt the margarine in the oven for 1 minute. Remove the sheet from the oven. Spread a layer of crushed digestive biscuits over the sheet.

Cover this layer with a layer of shredded coconut.

Cover with a layer of chocolate chips.

Finally, pour the condensed milk over.

Bake for about 20 minutes until golden brown.

Remove from the oven and add the walnuts and porridge oats, gently pressing them into the mixture before it cools. Allow to cool on the sheet and cut the mixture into individual bars.

Pack individually in foil. Eat within a week or so, or freeze until required.

# Granny's muesli bars

Marshmallows are the key ingredient here. They are a great comfort food. They are also light, they keep well and you can eat them on the route. Try cooking with them as below or roasting them on sticks around the campfire.

Makes 12 bars    Prep. time: 10 mins

| | |
|---|---|
| **3 tbsp** | **margarine** |
| **280-g** | **packet marshmallows** |
| **2 cups/300 g** | **mixed nuts and raisins** |
| **2 cups/50 g** | **corn flakes or rice cereal** |
| **2 cups/240 g** | **muesli** |

### At home:

In a large pan, melt the margarine and slowly add the marshmallows.

Heat very gently until the mixture is completely melted.

Stir in the nuts and raisins, cereal and muesli and combine all the ingredients.

Pour onto a 35 x 25-cm baking sheet and spread the mixture evenly.

Allow to stand for 15 minutes and cut into bars.

Wrap each bar individually. Granny's muesli bars are best eaten within four days.

# Carrot and date bar

A lovely combination of flavours, tastes and textures and packed with goodness. When cooking with honey, first rub a film of oil on your spoon to prevent the honey sticking – it will slide off easily. Another method is to dip your spoon or cup into flour first.

Makes 16 bars   Prep. time: 15 mins   Cooking time: 30 mins

| | |
|---|---|
| **1 cup/110 g** | **wholewheat flour** |
| **1 tsp** | **baking powder** |
| **1/2 tsp** | **salt** |
| **2** | **eggs** |
| **cup** | **honey** |
| **1 cup/225 g** | **chopped dates** |
| **1 cup/150 g** | **finely shredded carrot** |
| **cup/75 g** | **chopped walnuts** |

## At home:

Pre-heat the oven to 180°C/350°F. Grease a 25 x 25-cm baking pan.

In a large bowl, mix the flour, baking powder and salt. In a second bowl beat the eggs and honey together. Then slowly add the flour mixture and blend well.

Add the dates, carrot and nuts and mix well. Spoon the mixture into the baking pan and spread evenly. Bake for 30 minutes or until golden brown.

Remove from the oven and allow to cool in the pan before cutting into bars. Pack in airtight bags and store in a cool place if you plan to eat them within a few days, otherwise store in the frigde until required.

# Fruit balls

If you need a quick energy fix or just want a mouthful of flavour, pop in a fruit ball. You can use any dried fruits, although apricots work really well because of their high sugar content.

Makes 16 Prep. time: 10 mins

| | |
|---|---|
| **3/4 cup/110 g** | **dried apricots or other dried fruit** |
| **1 cup/75 g** | **shredded coconut** |
| **1/2 cup/120 ml** | **condensed milk** |
| **2 tbsp** | **icing sugar** |

## At home:

In a large bowl, mix the fruit and coconut. Pour in the milk and blend well. Shape into balls (about 16) and roll in the sugar to coat. Pack in airtight bags.

# Chocolate kickers

If you start to flag towards the end of the day, pop one of these energy-packed balls into your mouth and you'll find you've got a new spring in your step. A delicious treat that can be made before you leave, or at camp.

Makes 15 bite-sized balls Prep. time: 15 mins

| | |
|---|---|
| **1 cup/100 g** | **icing sugar** |
| **1 cup/255 g** | **crunchy peanut butter** |
| **1 cup/225 g** | **dark or semi-sweet chocolate chips** |
| **1/2 cup/115 g** | **powdered milk** |
| **2 tbsp** | **water** |

## At home:

Mix all the ingredients together in a large bowl and shape into bite-sized balls. Allow to stand for 15 minutes and pack into airtight bags.

# Nutty oat cookies

This is an easy way to make biscuits on the way without having to do any cooking. All you have to do is a little mixing and boil some water.

Makes 12 Prep. time: 10 mins

| | |
|---|---|
| **2 tbsp** | **butter or margarine** |
| **1/4 cup/60 g** | **powdered drinking chocolate** |
| **1 1/2 cups/135 g** | **porridge oats** |
| **2 tbsp** | **powdered milk** |
| **1/4 tsp** | **salt** |
| **3 tbsp** | **peanut butter** |
| **1/3 cup/65 g** | **sugar** |

## At camp:

Heat 1/4 cup of water in a large pan. Add the butter and drinking chocolate and bring to the boil. Add all the remaining ingredients except the sugar and mix well.
Shape the mixture into balls (about 12), flatten them onto a sheet and sprinkle with sugar. Pack in airtight bags and store in a cool, dark place. They will keep for about a week. If you want to keep them longer, they will need to be refrigerated.

# Pam's nuts

A delicious and nutritious nutty snack that is great for on-the-move food – or even when watching TV back home.

Serves 2  Prep. time: 10 mins  Cooking time: 20 mins

| | |
|---|---|
| **3 tsp** | **salt** |
| **1/2 tsp** | **cayenne pepper** |
| **1/2 tsp** | **white pepper** |
| **1/2 tsp** | **ground nutmeg** |
| **1/2 tsp** | **ground allspice** |
| **4 cups/600 g** | **assorted unsalted, shelled nuts (such as peanuts, cashews, pecans, walnut pieces, almonds)** |
| **4 tbsp** | **butter** |
| **1/2 cup/120 g** | **maple syrup, light molasses or treacle** |

## At home:

Preheat the oven to 180ºC/350ºF. Place all the seasonings in a large bowl, add the nuts and mix to combine.

In a pan over a medium heat, melt the butter and add it to the mixture. Stir all the ingredients until they are well combined.

Place the mixture on a 35 x 25-cm baking sheet and bake in the oven until roasted, about 10 minutes. Stir occasionally to prevent sticking.

Put the roasted nuts back into the bowl and add the maple syrup and stir to coat the nuts.

Return the mixture to the baking sheet and bake for a further 10 minutes, until the nuts have a darkish, glazed appearance.

Allow to cool and then pack into airtight containers.

# Fruit cocktail

A thirst-quenching drink any time. Great for breakfast, lunch or dinner and a great reviver at the end of a long day on the track.

Serves 4

| | |
|---|---|
| **1 cup/240 ml** | **orange juice** |
| **1 cup/240 ml** | **pineapple juice** |
| **1 cup/240 ml** | **grapefruit juice** |
| **1 cup/240 ml** | **cranberry juice** |

Simply combine all the juices and bottle. Shake well before serving.
Keep in an airtight container and this drink will be good for several days.

# Lemonade

A wonderfully refreshing drink that can be sweetened to suit your taste.
This lemonade is at its best chilled. Simply place in a seal-tight container and immerse in cool water or, if you have a cooler, even better.
However, it's also soothingly refreshing when served warm.

Serves 4

| | |
|---|---|
| **1 cup/240 ml** | **lemon juice** |
| **4 tsp** | **sugar** |
| **4 cups/960 ml** | **water** |

Combine the lemon juice with the sugar in a large sealed container and stir until the sugar is dissolved. Add the water, stir and serve.

## Spicy hot chocolate

A really decadent hot drink for those special moments when life under canvas needs spicing up and for when you need a sugar hit. This is the perfect drink for chocaholics.

Serves 6 Prep./cooking time: 10 mins

| | |
|---|---|
| **2 x 110-g** | **bars dark or milk chocolate** |
| **4 cups/960 ml** | **water** |
| **400-g** | **can condensed milk** |
| **pinch** | **cayenne pepper** |
| **1/2 tsp** | **cinnamon** |

Break the chocolate into small pieces. Boil the water in a pan and add the chocolate and milk. Stir over a medium heat until all the chocolate has melted. Add the cayenne. Serve sprinkled with cinnamon.

## Spiced tea

Tea is always invigorating and this spiced-up version is even more refreshing, especially at the end of a long, tiring day.

Serves 8

| | |
|---|---|
| **1/2 cup/100 g** | **sugar** |
| **8** | **tea bags** |
| **6** | **cloves** |
| **1** | **cinnamon stick** |
| | **strips of orange rind** |

In a pan over a gentle heat, melt the sugar in 3/4 cup of water to produce a syrup.
Make up the tea in 4 cups of water.
Remove the sugar syrup from the heat and add the cloves, cinnamon stick and orange rind. Pour into the hot tea, stir and serve piping hot.

# Rose hip tea

Rose hips are the fruit of the wild rose and some garden roses and can be gathered at the end of summer, or obtained from health stores or herbal suppliers.

| | |
|---|---|
| **3 to 4 tbsp** | **fresh rose hips per cup** |

Boil the water, remove from the heat and add the rose hips. Steep for 15 to 20 minutes. Serve with honey to sweeten, as desired.

# Beef tea

A quick, warming and nutritious pick-me-up anywhere, anytime.

Add boiling water to mugs containing 2 teaspoons each of Marmite, Bovril, Vegemite or 2 beef bouillion cubes

# Ginger water

Ginger water is a wonderful thirst-quencher, as well as a good remedy for upset stomachs and nausea. It is best to use fresh ginger, peeled and grated – fresh ginger keeps for several days so it is useful for a number of recipes.

Serves 6

| | |
|---|---|
| **10-cm** | **piece fresh ginger, peeled and grated.** |
| **3/4 cup/150 g** | **sugar** |
| **4 cups/960 ml** | **water** |
| **1** | **orange, peeled and sliced** |

Mix the grated ginger, sugar and water together in a sealed container and leave to stand for 6 hours. Immerse the container in a cold-water stream or lake, as this drink is best served chilled. To serve, strain to remove the pulp and ginger, and pour into mugs. Decorate with orange slices.

# Chocolate coffee

This is the perfect drink for chocolate and caffeine addicts. Drink it warm and it makes a great after-dinner drink or nightcap. Drink it cold and it is perfect at lunch on a hot summer's day. Two or three black cherries added to the mug is a special treat.

Serves 2

| | |
|---|---|
| **2 cups/480 ml** | **water** |
| **2 tbsp** | **fresh coffee grounds** |
| **110-g** | **bar dark chocolate, broken into pieces** |

Boil the water in a pan, add the coffee grounds and stir. Remove from the heat and add the chocolate, piece by piece, and stir until melted.
Pour into mugs, using a spoon to hold back the coffee grounds.

# Camp coffee

The first thing the first person to wake up should do is put on the coffee.

One of the quickest, most efficient and delicious ways to make a large pot of camp coffee is to boil the water in a big pot for 5 minutes.

Add 1 tsp coffee per cup, boil it up again for 2 to 3 more minutes, then take the pot off the heat and leave it to stand for 1 minute.

Dribble half a cup cold water along the surface, tap the pot repeatedly with a metal utensil for about 30 seconds to make the grounds sink to the bottom. Let the coffee settle for another minute, and then pour hot steaming coffee gently from the top.

# Breakfasts

Breakfast is the most important meal of the day because it packs in the fuel you will need on the route. We are also of the firm belief that it should be an enjoyable meal. There is no reason why you should eat a bowl of cereal every day – no matter how good this may be for you. Be adventurous and you'll be amazed by what you can create.

# Porridge surprise

Add different ingredients whenever you serve this nutritious bowl. Apart from using a range of fruits, both dried and fresh, you can use different toppings – honey, syrup and one of our favourite combinations – cranberry and brown sugar.

Serves 4 Prep. time: 5 mins Cooking time: less than 5 mins

| | |
|---|---|
| **3 cups/720 ml** | **milk or reconstituted powdered milk** |
| **1 1/2 cups/135 g** | **porridge oats** |
| **1 cup/150 g** | **dried cranberries** |
| **1 tsp** | **brown sugar** |
| **pinch** | **cinnamon** |

### At camp:

Bring the milk to the boil in a large pan. Add the oatmeal and cook for 5 minutes, stirring occasionally. Remove from the heat, add the cranberries and brown sugar and mix well. Serve with a sprinkling of cinnamon.

# Fruit treat

Serves 2 Prep. time: 2 mins Cooking time: 3–4 mins

| | |
|---|---|
| **1/2 cup/75 g** | **chopped dried apricots** |
| **3 cups/720 ml** | **water** |
| **1/2 cup/80 g** | **raisins** |
| **1/2 tsp** | **salt** |
| **1 cup/70 g** | **powdered milk** |
| **225-g** | **can creamed rice** |
| **1/4 cup/45 g** | **brown sugar** |

### At camp:

Place the apricots and water in a pan and bring to the boil. Gradually stir in the remaining ingredients, bring back to the boil and cook for 1 minute, stirring frequently. Remove from the heat, cover with a lid and stand for 5 minutes, then pour into bowls to serve.

# Banana pancakes

This recipe is quick and easy to prepare and provides a delicious, healthy, energy-packed breakfast. You can substitute other fruits for the bananas.

Serves 6 (2 pancakes each) Prep. time: 5 mins
Cooking time: 10–15 mins for the complete batch

| | |
|---|---|
| **2 cups/220 g** | **plain flour** |
| **1 tsp** | **salt** |
| **2 tbsp** | **sugar** |
| **1 tsp** | **bicarbonate of soda** |
| **2** | **eggs or egg powder equivalent** |
| **2 cups/480 ml** | **milk or reconstituted powdered milk** |
| **3 tbsp** | **butter** |
| **1** | **banana, finely sliced** |
| **1 tbsp** | **vegetable oil** |

## At camp:

In a large bowl, mix together the flour, salt, sugar and bicarbonate of soda. In a smaller bowl, mix the eggs, milk and butter. Blend in the dry mixture to form a batter. Gradually add the sliced banana to the mix.

Heat a skillet over a medium heat, add a little oil to prevent sticking, and pour in about 2 tablespoons of batter for each pancake. Serve with jams or other preserves.

# Scrambled eggs 'n' coffee

Cook your eggs while you make your coffee. It's simple and economical on fuel and time. When your eggs are cooked, place them on to a plate and pour a cup of coffee. This is the fastest way to cook breakfast and the best thing about it is that it makes great, fluffy scrambled eggs.

Serves **2** Prep. time: **5** mins Cooking time: **10** mins

| | |
|---|---|
| **4** | **eggs or egg powder equivalent** |
| **3 tbsp** | **milk or reconstituted powdered milk** |
| | **salt and pepper, to taste** |

## At camp:

Boil water in a pan or coffee pot. Crack the eggs into a plastic bag, add the milk and season to taste.

Pop the bag into the boiling water for a few minutes and then remove and check your eggs. If the eggs look cooked i.e., there is no liquid in the bag, keep the bag closed and use your fingers to scramble them through the bag. Open the bag and serve.

You could add a little cheese to the eggs in the initial mix or sprinkle some on the eggs on the plate.

# Country no-crust quiche

If you plan a lazy morning and leisurely breakfast, then you can find things to do around the campsite while this quiche cooks in the Dutch oven – it will be worth the wait and you can finish it off cold for lunch.

Serves 6 Prep. time: 10 mins Cooking time: 30–45 mins

| | |
|---|---|
| **1 tbsp** | **butter** |
| **1 tbsp** | **plain flour** |
| **1 cup** | **grated cheddar or gruyere cheese** |
| **4** | **eggs or egg powder equivalent** |
| **1$^1/_2$ cups/360 ml** | **milk or single cream** |
| **1 tbsp** | **chopped herbs (fresh or dried)** |
| **$^1/_2$ tsp** | **salt** |
| **pinch** | **nutmeg** |
| **pinch** | **pepper** |

## At camp:

Line a Dutch oven with foil and grease with butter Bring to a medium heat.

Put the flour in a bag, add the cheese and toss to coat in the flour.

In a bowl, beat the eggs and add the milk, herbs, salt, nutmeg and pepper.

Add the coated cheese to the egg mixture and pour into the Dutch oven.

Bake until set. Remove from the oven, allow to rest for 10 minutes then slice and serve.

# Omelette in a bag

Serves 1 Prep. time: 2 mins Cooking time: less than 5 mins

| | |
|---|---|
| **2** | **eggs** |
| **1 tbsp** | **grated cheese** |
| **1 tbsp** | **diced ham, optional** |
| **1 tbsp** | **diced peppers, optional** |
| **1 tbsp** | **diced tomatoes, optional** |
| | **salt and pepper, to taste** |

### At camp:

Set a large pan of water to boil. Crack the eggs into a large, sealable plastic bag and add the remaining ingredients. Seal the bag and then squish it with your fingers so that the contents are well mixed. Place the bag in the pot of boiling water and cook for 3 or 4 minutes, stirring occasionally.

The eggs are cooked when there is no longer any liquid in the bag.

To serve, open the bag and slip the omelette onto a plate

# Bacon and eggs on a bagel

Bacon keeps well if pre-cooked and sealed in plastic wrap. It will last for four or five days under most conditions and can be reheated in a frying pan.

Serves 2 Prep. time: 5 mins Cooking time: 5 mins

| | |
|---|---|
| **4** | **rashers pre-cooked bacon** |
| **2** | **eggs or egg powder equivalent** |
| **1 tbsp** | **butter or margarine** |
| **2** | **bagels** |
| | **salt and pepper, to taste** |

### At camp:

Make scrambled eggs (see page 68), re-heat the bacon and serve with the eggs on both halves of a buttered sliced bagel.

# French toast

This is a very easy, tasty and filling breakfast and a great way to use up any old bread as well.

Serves 2 (3 slices each) Prep. time: 2–3 mins Cooking time: 15 mins

| | |
|---|---|
| **2** | **eggs or egg powder equivalent** |
| **1/2 cup** | **milk or reconstituted powdered milk** |
| **3 drops** | **vanilla extract** |
| **pinch** | **cinnamon, optional** |
| **6** | **thick slices white bread** |
| **4 tbsp** | **butter or margarine** |

## At camp:

Break the eggs into a bowl and add the milk, vanilla and cinnamon. Dip the slices of bread into the mixture, to thoroughly coat both sides.

Melt a little of the butter in a hot skillet. Add a bread to the pan, a slice at a time. Cook each side for 2 to 3 minutes, until golden brown. Add more butter or margarine as needed.

Serve with jam, honey or maple syrup.

# All-day breakfast

Serves 2 Prep. time: 5 mins Cooking time: 10 mins

| | |
|---|---|
| ✪ 6 | **sausage links or small sausages** |
| ✪ 1 | **potato** |
| 6 | **eggs or reconstituted egg powder equivalent** |
| 3 tbsp | **milk or reconstituted powdered milk** |
| ✪ 75 g | **chopped mushrooms** |
| 55 g | **grated cheese** |
| | **salt and pepper, to taste** |

## At camp:

In a frying pan or skillet, fry the sausages for 10 minutes, until they are cooked through. While the sausages are cooking, peel and finely dice the potato. When the sausages are cooked, remove them from the pan and cut into bite-sized pieces. In the fat remaining in the pan, cook the diced potato until soft and golden. Beat the eggs, mix in the milk and pour the mixture over the potato. As the eggs are cooking, add the mushrooms and grated cheese, and season to taste. Serve as the cheese melts.

# Breakfast casserole

This Dutch-oven breakfast is sometimes referred to as the cholesterol casserole – for obvious reasons. It does taste very good though!

Serves 4 hungry campers Prep. time: 10 mins Cooking time: 40 mins

| | |
|---|---|
| **1 tbsp** | **butter** |
| **4** | **thick slices white bread** |
| **455 g** | **cooked sausage patties or cooked sausage meat** |
| **1 cup** | **grated cheddar cheese** |
| **6** | **eggs or egg powder equivalent** |
| **2 cups/480 ml** | **milk or reconstituted powdered milk** |
| **1 tsp** | **mustard powder** |
| | **salt, to taste** |

## At camp:

Line a Dutch oven with foil and grease with butter. Break up the bread and form a base in the bottom of the oven. Crumble the sausage over the bread and cover with the cheese.

In a bowl, lightly beat the eggs, milk and mustard and season to taste. Pour this mixture over the cheese. Cover and bake for 35 to 40 minutes. As it cooks, the cheese rises to the top and forms a golden crust over a layer of eggs. Make sure it does not cook too fast and that the eggs are cooked through to your liking.

# Soups, snacks & lunches

If you are enjoying a leisurely circular walk you will have the luxury of stopping for lunch and rustling something up. If you are trying to cover a set distance every day, a short stop will give you enough time to heat up some soup or tuck into a tasty snack. Either way, we hope you will find something to tempt you in the following pages.

# Chickpea and pasta soup

Sometimes it is good to take a lingering and leisurely lunch and this is the ideal soup for those occasions.

Makes 4 large helpings  Prep. time: 5 mins  Cooking time: 30 mins

| | |
|---|---|
| **1 tbsp** | **olive oil** |
| **4** | **cloves garlic, crushed** |
| **1 tbsp** | **chopped fresh rosemary** |
| **400-g** | **can chopped tomatoes** |
| **2 cups/480 ml** | **chicken stock, or 3 chicken stock cubes in 2 cups/480 ml water** |
| **1 cup/200 g** | **canned chickpeas** |
| **1 cup/85 g** | **pasta (such as macaroni or fusilli)** |

## At camp:

Heat the oil in a large pot over a medium heat. Add the garlic and sauté gently for 3 to 4 minutes, stirring frequently to prevent the garlic from burning. Add the rosemary and cook for a further 2 minutes. Add the tomatoes, cover and simmer for 15 minutes. Add the stock and simmer, covered, for another 10 minutes. Finally, add the chickpeas, pasta, season and cook for a further 8 to 10 minutes, until *al dente*.

# Swedish apple soup

This is a thick gazpacho-type soup and it is very refreshing and convenient for lunch. It must be prepared at home and is best eaten cold.

Serves 4 Prep. time: 10 mins Cooking time: 45 mins

| | |
|---|---|
| **6** | **dessert apples, peeled, cored and sliced** |
| **2** | **cloves** |
| **1 tbsp** | **sugar** |
| **1 tbsp** | **cinnamon** |
| **6 tbsp** | **butter, melted** |
| **1 cup/200 g** | **sugar** |
| **1 cup/120 g** | **plain flour** |
| **1** | **egg or egg powder equivalent** |
| **2–3 drops** | **vanilla extract** |
| | **salt, to taste** |

## At home:

Pre-heat the oven to 180°C/350°F. Grease a 23-cm pie dish and build up layers of apple slices until the disk is about two-thirds full. Add the cloves and sprinkle with 1 tablespoon sugar and the cinnamon.

In a bowl, thoroughly combine the butter, remaining sugar, flour, egg, vanilla and a little salt to taste. Pour over the apples and bake for about 45 minutes. Allow to cool completely then store in airtight bags or containers.

# Summa' soup

This lunch is best served towards the end of your trip as it allows you to use up any leftovers – hence the name: summa' this and summa' that! Always have the basic ingredients such as beef, chicken or vegetable stock cubes, herbs and spices with you to get things going.

Serves 4 Prep. time: 5 mins Cooking time: 10 mins

| | |
|---|---|
| **1 cup/150 g** | **diced assorted vegetables** |
| **4** | **stock cubes** |
| | **dried herbs, to taste** |
| | **salt and pepper, to taste** |
| **2 cups/380 g** | **rice, noodles or couscous** |

### At home:

Dehydrate the vegetables and pack in an airtight bag (see p. 19).

### At camp:

Boil 950 ml water and crumble in the stock cubes. Add herbs and season to taste.
Reduce the heat and add whatever left-over vegetables and meats are available.
Use spaghetti and you have minestrone-style soup.
Use vegetable stock and add beans, noodles and left-overs to make a rich vegetable bean soup.
Use beef stock cubes, add a little milk and mushrooms plus left-overs and rice and you have a stroganoff-beef and mushroom combination.
When using left-overs, always warm them thoroughly but don't let the water boil or everything will become mushy. Simmering the contents will ensure they are hot when served and that any bacteria have been destroyed.

# Pitta fillings

Be adventurous when it comes to pitta fillings. Here are some suggestions to brighten a pitta sandwich.

Mix together some diced, cooked chicken breast, finely sliced onion and 1 tsp of salsa to make a Mexican pitta.

Toss cooked chicken cubes in natural yoghurt with a pinch of finely chopped fresh mint to make a refreshing Greek-style pitta.

Mix up chopped, raw mushrooms, aubergine and feta cheese for an interesting vegetarian bite.

# Pitta pizza

This is a fun lunch that is quick to prepare. You can improvise and add your favourite toppings.

Serves 2 Prep. time: 5 mins Cooking time: 8–10 mins

| | |
|---|---|
| **2** | **pitta breads** |
| **1/2 cup/120 ml** | **tomato and basil sauce (p. 98)** |
| **60 g** | **thinly sliced salami** |
| **1/2 cup/55 g** | **grated cheddar cheese** |

## At camp:

Put the pitta breads in a large skillet and cover them with the tomato and basil sauce. Move the pittas occasionally to prevent them sticking or burning.
Layer with slices of salami. Sprinkle on the grated cheese. Heat gently until the cheese is melted and you have a freshly made pitta pizza.

# Tomato, cucumber and red onion salad

A really easy salad to make, but do plan ahead here because it needs about an hour for all the ingredients to blend. However, it is worth that wait.

Serves 6 Prep. time: 10 mins Standing time: 1 hour

| | |
|---|---|
| **2** | **cucumbers** |
| **1/3 cup** | **red wine vinegar** |
| **1 tbsp** | **sugar** |
| **1 tsp** | **salt** |
| **3** | **tomatoes, de-seeded and chopped (not too finely)** |
| **1** | **red onion, chopped** |
| **small bunch** | **fresh mint, chopped** |
| **3 tbsp** | **oil** |
| | **salt and pepper, to taste** |

## At camp:

Peel the cucumbers and slice them in half lengthways, de-seed and slice across.
In a large bowl, mix together the cucumber, vinegar, sugar and salt. Leave to stand for about 1 hour, during which time you can chop the remaining ingredients.
When you are ready to serve, add the tomatoes, onion, mint and oil, and toss. Season with salt and pepper to taste.

## Trailside tips:

- If your trip is over several weeks and you plan to visit some towns, pack special provisions that can be mailed to yourself at a point on your itinerary. This will top up supplies less readily available, or refresh your meal ideas.
- Save fuel by undercooking foods slightly and letting them sit for a few moments, covered, to finish cooking. This works best with vegetables.
- It's always a nice idea to pack a 'surprise' treat to pull out of the pack when your party least expects it, and perhaps most needs it. Liquorice, peanuts and raisins or sweets – high energy, high morale!

# On the go apple 'n' nut snack

This is a clever way of packing the calories in while on the move and has been a Boy Scout staple for decades.

Serves **2** Prep. time: **3** mins

| | |
|---|---|
| **2 tbsp** | **peanut butter** |
| **2 tbsp** | **peanuts** |
| **2 tbsp** | **raisins and/or chocolate chips** |
| **2** | **apples** |

## At camp:

Mix the peanut butter, peanuts, raisins and/or chocolate chips into a sticky paste. Core the apples and stuff the holes with the paste. If there is any paste left over, enjoy as a perk for the cook. Wrap each apple in plastic wrap or in a plastic bag with as much air squeezed out as possible. Keep in your pocket or backpack until you feel like a bite.

# Black bean spread

Dips and spreads are made for eating along the path with bread or crackers, and robust flavours are what you need when eating outdoors. This spread is very tasty and nutritious and can be prepared ahead.

Serves 6 (over 2 lunches)  Prep. time: 5 mins

| | |
|---|---|
| **400-g** | **can black beans** |
| **2** | **cloves garlic, crushed** |
| **4 tbsp** | **hot or medium salsa** |
| **1/2 cup/110 g** | **cottage cheese** |
| **1 tsp** | **hot pepper sauce, optional** |
| **2 tsp** | **ground cumin** |
| **1 tsp** | **chopped fresh coriander** |
| | **salt and pepper, to taste** |

## At home:

Drain the beans of their liquid and place them in a blender with all the other ingredients. Blend until smooth.

Pack in two airtight containers; each one should provide enough dip for six people. Refrigerate until required. On the route, eat it on the first day unless you can keep it in a cooler.

## Or at camp:

Drain the beans and place in bowl with all the other ingredients.

Use a fork, first to crush all ingredients and then to mix them into as smooth a paste as possible.

# Bacon and cheddar spread

Tasty and crunchy, this spread is sublime on hot bread in the great outdoors.

Serves **8** Prep. time: **15** mins Cooking time: **5** mins

| | |
|---|---|
| **10** | **rashers bacon** |
| **2 cups/225 g** | **grated cheddar cheese** |
| **1 tbsp** | **grated red onion** |
| **1 cup/240 ml** | **salad dressing (bought or home-made – see recipe below)** |

## At camp:

Fry the bacon in a skillet over medium heat until well cooked and crispy.

Drain and crumble into pieces.

In a bowl, mix the bacon, cheese, onion and dressing thoroughly. Serve on bread or crackers. If you are able, it is good chilled for an hour before serving.

# Instant creamy salad dressing

| | |
|---|---|
| **1/2** | **clove garlic, crushed** |
| **1/2 tbsp** | **oil** |
| **1/2 cup/120 ml** | **sour cream** |
| **1/4 cup** | **milk** |

## At camp:

Soften the garlic in a pan with the oil over a low heat for about 1 minute.

Add the soured cream and milk. Stir frequently until the mixture thickens.

Do not let it boil. Use immediately.

# Pasta bowl

This is fast food for a filling lunch. On a cold day, it is great to stop for a hot lunch and this one warms you down to your socks.

Serves 4 Prep. time: 5 mins Cooking time: 20 mins

| | |
|---|---|
| **1 cup/140 g** | **dried pasta (such as conchiole or macaroni)** |
| **1** | **green pepper, chopped** |
| **1** | **tomato, chopped** |
| **1** | **onion, finely chopped** |
| **400-g** | **can kidney beans** |
| **2 cups/480 ml** | **chicken stock** |
| **235-g** | **can chickpeas** |
| **1 tsp** | **Worcestershire sauce** |
| **1 tsp** | **dried basil** |
| **1** | **clove garlic, finely chopped** |

## At home:

Save time by mixing together the dry and dehydrated ingredients in one bag. Re-pack the canned beans in sealable plastic bags.

## At camp:

Mix together all the ingredients in a large pan, cover and bring to the boil.

Simmer for 15 minutes, stirring occasionally, until the pasta is *al dente*. You can add an extra 1/2 cup of pasta if you want to thicken the dish up.

# Speedy pasta

If you need an energy-packed meal but don't have too much time, put on a pan of water to boil, and make this speedy hi-carbo dish. It can be prepared in about 15 minutes and tastes great.

Serves **2** Prep. time: **15** minutes Cooking time: **10** mins.

| | |
|---|---|
| **1/2 tsp** | **salt** |
| **1 cup/85 g** | **pasta (such as penne or rigatoni)** |
| **1 tbsp** | **oil** |
| **1 cup/45 g** | **grated Parmesan** |
| **3** | **tomatoes, chopped** |
| **2 tsp** | **dried basil** |
| **1 tsp** | **dried parsley** |

## At camp:

Bring a large pot of salted water to the boil, add the pasta and cook on a gentle rolling boil for 7 minutes. When cooked *al dente*, remove from the heat and drain.

Add the oil, Parmesan, tomatoes and herbs. Toss everything together to coat the pasta and serve immediately. Grate or sprinkle over some extra Parmesan.

# No-pot stew

This is a simple but filling stew cooked in the bag so that no pots need to be washed up afterwards. It's a versatile dish because you can add almost anything to it.

Serves 4 Prep. time: 5 mins Cooking time: 30 mins.

| | |
|---|---|
| 2 | **large onions, sliced** |
| 1 | **large green pepper, sliced** |
| 2 | **large carrots, chopped into small chunks** |
| 2 | **potatoes, peeled and chopped into small chunks** |
| | **chopped sausage, leftover diced chicken, etc.** |
| 2 | **cloves garlic, crushed** |
| 1 tbsp | **butter or margarine** |
| | **salt and pepper, to taste** |

## At camp:

Place the vegetables and meat on a sheet of foil, smear with the crushed garlic and butter, and add salt and pepper to taste. Sprinkle with a little water, then fold the foil into a packet. Suspend above the campfire flames (not in direct contact) for about 30 minutes. If using uncooked meat, ensure it is fully cooked. Serve the stew with rice or noodles.

# Apple and turkey stir-fry

The great advantage of stir-fry is that you can prepare a quick, light meal that is full of flavour and is healthy and nutritious. If you do a little preparation after breakfast, you can rustle up this lunch in less than 15 minutes.

Serves 6 Prep. time: 5 mins (standing time 30 mins) Cooking time: 7–9 mins

| | |
|---|---|
| **1/2 tsp** | **ground black pepper** |
| **2** | **cloves garlic, crushed** |
| **1 tbsp** | **brown sugar** |
| **2 tbsp** | **soy sauce** |
| **1 tbsp** | **Worcestershire sauce** |
| **1 tbsp** | **cornflour** |
| **1/2 cup/120 ml** | **unsweetened apple juice** |
| **680 g** | **turkey breast, diced** |
| **1 tbsp** | **oil** |
| **1 cup/150 g** | **mange tout/snowpeas** |
| **4** | **carrots, finely chopped** |

## At camp:

Mix together the pepper, garlic, sugar, soy sauce, Worcestershire sauce, cornflour and apple juice in a large, plastic, sealable bag. Add the diced turkey. You can do this in camp before heading out for the day.

When you stop for lunch, heat the oil in a pan over a high heat. Add the turkey mixture and stir-fry for 5 or 6 minutes. As the turkey cooks, push it to the sides of the pan and add the vegetables in the centre and cook for a further 3 minutes.

Serve the turkey and vegetables alone or with rice.

# Fruit log

Because this finger food has a high sugar content, it will keep well for several days if you make it in advance. However, it is quick and simple enough to throw together in a few moments in the camp kitchen.

Makes 10 slices   Prep. time: 15 mins.

| | |
|---|---|
| **1/2 cup/120 g** | **chopped dates** |
| **1/2 cup/80 g** | **chopped raisins** |
| **1/2 cup/40 g** | **shredded coconut** |
| **1/2 cup/75 g** | **chopped mixed nuts** |
| **1/2 cup/115 g** | **glacé cherries, chopped,** |
| **1/2 cup/75 g** | **chopped dried apricots** |
| **1/2 cup/75 g** | **chopped peaches (fresh or canned)** |
| **1/4 cup/60 g** | **chopped dried figs** |
| **2 tbsp** | **orange juice** |
| **1 tbsp** | **icing sugar** |

## At home:

Make sure that all the fruits and nuts are chopped as finely as possible and mix them altogether in a large bowl. Stir in the orange juice and then with your hands, thoroughly bind this mixture together. Lift the mixture out onto a board and form it into the shape of a log about 20–25 cm long and 10 cm in diameter. Sprinkle with the sugar.

(An alternative is to omit the mixed nuts from the mixture and instead roll the finished log over the nuts to coat.)

Pack the log in an airtight plastic bag or slice into portions and wrap individually. Refrigerate until needed, but if packed in airtight bags this log will keep for many days on the track – assuming you can resist the temptation to eat it sooner!

# Peanut crisp

Peanuts are packed with energy and by the time you have added the honey, sugar and fruit, you will have no trouble striding out all afternoon.

Serves 6  Prep. time: 10 mins  Cooking time: 10 mins

| | |
|---|---|
| **1 tbsp** | **margarine** |
| **1/4 cup/90 g** | **brown sugar** |
| **2 tbsp** | **honey** |
| **1/2 cup/130 g** | **crunchy peanut butter** |
| **1 1/4 cups/30 g** | **cereal flakes** |
| **3 tbsp** | **assorted mixed dried fruits** |

## At camp:

Grease a 35 x 23-cm baking sheet with margarine

Place the sugar and honey in a medium-sized pan and stir over a medium heat until the sugar is dissolved. Watch it continuously to ensure it does not burn. Remove from the heat and stir in the peanut butter, combining until the mixture is smooth. Add the cereal flakes and dried fruits.

Spread the mixture over the baking sheet about 2.5 cm deep. When cool, cut the peanut crisp into squares to serve, or seal in plastic wrap for individual packing.

# One-pot suppers & sides

Nutritionally, dinner is the most important meal of the day after breakfast. When trekking, you are usually tired, footsore and certainly hungry by dinnertime, and it's often difficult to muster up the energy to prepare a decent meal. However, it is a good idea to refuel your body overnight to keep warm and rehydrated. The following recipes are devised not only to be nutritious, they are all temptingly quick to make. One-pot suppers are made with the minimum of fuss and adding a variety of sides will turn your camp meal into a 'psychological' banquet.

# Lentil chilli

This is a great-tasting and nutritious vegetable chilli. Bulghur wheat has all the nutrients of wholewheat, but adds bulk and doesn't need to be cooked for so long.

Serves 6 Prep. time: 10 mins Cooking time: 35 mins

| | |
|---|---|
| **2 tbsp** | **oil** |
| **1** | **large onion, finely chopped** |
| **1** | **green pepper, chopped** |
| **4** | **cloves garlic, crushed** |
| **1 cup/200 g** | **dried lentils** |
| **1 cup/230 g** | **bulghur wheat** |
| **3** | **large potatoes, peeled and cut into small cubes** |
| **3 cups/720 ml** | **vegetable stock** |
| **450-g** | **can chopped tomatoes** |
| **2 tsp** | **chilli powder** |
| **1 tbsp** | **ground cumin** |

## At camp:

Heat the oil in a large pot over a medium heat. Add the onion, pepper and garlic and sauté for 5 minutes until softened. Stir in the remaining ingredients.

Bring the mixture to the boil, cover and simmer gently for 30 minutes, stirring occasionally, until the lentils are tender. Serve immediately while piping hot in bowls.

# Chicken and apple stew

This makes a very nutritious stew and you can add additional favourite vegetables if you wish. Ideally, this is made in a Dutch oven but you can make it in a pan on a camping stove as long as you have plenty of fuel.

Serves 4 Prep. time: 10 mins Cooking time: 45 mins

| | |
|---|---|
| **1 tbsp** | **oil** |
| **450 g** | **skinless chicken breast, cut into cubes** |
| **pinch** | **nutmeg** |
| | **salt and pepper, to taste** |
| **1 tbsp** | **Dijon mustard** |
| **475 ml** | **chicken stock (or use 3 chicken stock cubes dissolved in water)** |
| **1/4 cup** | **apple cider vinegar** |
| **4** | **cloves** |
| **1** | **potato, peeled and cut into small pieces** |
| **2** | **carrots, finely sliced** |
| **4** | **red apples, peeled, cored and cut into thick slices** |
| **1 cup/240 ml** | **unsweetened apple sauce** |

## At camp:

Heat the oil in a large pan over medium heat. Add the chicken and cook for about 5 minutes, turning frequently, until golden brown. Add the nutmeg, salt and pepper and the mustard. Stir to ensure the chicken is well coated. Add the stock, vinegar, cloves, potatoes and carrots.

Bring to the boil, cover and simmer gently for about 15 minutes.

Add the apples and cook for a further 15 minutes. Avoid overcooking the apples because you want them to retain shape and texture. Remove the meat and vegetables and keep them warm in a pot by the fire.

Add the apple sauce to the stock and boil for a further 5 minutes. Serve the chicken and vegetables in bowls, with the hot broth poured over.

# Pasta Alfredo

Alfredo sauce combines the richness of cream with the tanginess of Parmesan cheese – both ingredients that go wonderfully well with pasta. This is a delicious meal that can be rustled up while the rest of the gang put the tents up and light the fire.

Serves **8** Prep. time: **10** mins Cooking time: **10** mins

| | |
|---|---|
| **450 g** | **pasta (such as penne or rigatoni)** |
| **4 tbsp** | **butter or margarine** |
| **2 cups/140 g** | **sliced mushrooms** |
| **1/2 cup/120 ml** | **double cream** |
| **200 g** | **cooked ham, into thin strips** |
| **900 g** | **skinless, boneless chicken breasts, cut into cubes** |
| **2/3 cup** | **grated Parmesan** |
| | **ground black pepper, to taste** |

## In camp:

In a large pot, bring salted water to the boil and cook the pasta for 10 minutes, until it is *al dente*.

In a skillet melt half of the butter over medium heat and sauté the mushrooms until brown. Add the cream to the mushrooms and, stirring frequently, add the ham and chicken and heat through.

When the pasta is ready, remove it from the heat, drain, return to the pot and toss with the remaining butter and the mushroom mixture, stirring it around thoroughly to distribute the ingredients. Serve in large bowls with a sprinkling of Parmesan, and lots of black pepper.

# Dutch-oven lasagne

A delicious and easy-to-make camp 'lasagne'. It takes quite a long time to cook so is best made in a Dutch oven over the hot embers of a campfire.

This is not a meal for the lightweight camper but, if you are in a large group sharing the load or with a vehicle, it is well worth the effort.

Serves 8 to 12   Prep. time: 15 mins   Cooking time: 45 mins

| | |
|---|---|
| **900 g** | **ground beef** |
| | **tomato and basil sauce (see below)** |
| **2 cups/450 g** | **ricotta or cottage cheese** |
| **3** | **eggs or egg powder equivalent** |
| **1 tsp** | **dried oregano** |
| **1/2 tsp** | **dried basil** |
| **12** | **sheets oven-ready lasagne** |
| **450 g** | **grated cheddar cheese** |
| **25 g** | **grated Parmesan** |

### Tomato and basil sauce:

| | |
|---|---|
| **10** | **tomatoes** |
| **1/2 cup** | **fresh basil, finely chopped** |
| **6 tbsp** | **olive oil** |
| **4** | **cloves garlic, chopped** |
| | **salt and black pepper, to taste** |

### At home:

To make the tomato and basil sauce: De-seed and finely dice the tomatoes. Place in a large bowl, add the basil, oil, garlic and salt and pepper. Mix thoroughly and let stand for 1 hour before packing in an airtight container. Refrigerate. Use within a day or two.

### At camp:

Set a Dutch oven over the embers of a fire and pre-heat. Add the meat straight into the oven and seal in its juices until brown, about 5 to 6 minutes. Remove from the heat and set the meat aside in a bowl.

Add the tomato and basil sauce to the meat and mix thoroughly.

In a separate bowl, mix together the ricotta cheese, eggs and herbs.

Now line the base and sides of the oven with foil brushed with melted butter and return to the fire. Make sure the foil extends well up the sides of the oven.

### To assemble the lasagne:

Spread a layer of meat sauce evenly over the foil in the base of the oven. Cover with 3 sheets of lasagne. The pasta will expand during cooking, so the pieces need not overlap each other.

Spread a layer of ricotta cheese mixture on top of the lasagne sheets. Then layer another portion of meat sauce and a layer of cheddar cheese. Add more layers of lasagne, ricotta, meat sauce and cheddar until all except 1 cup of cheddar is used up. Sprinkle Parmesan over the top. Cover the lasagne with foil.

Cover with the lid of the oven and rake up some hot embers over the top. Bake for about 30 minutes.

Remove the lid and foil and sprinkle the remaining cheddar on top of the lasagne and bake for a further 10 minutes. Remove the oven from the fire, allow to stand for about 5 minutes and lift out the lasagne. Let it stand for a few minutes after which it is easier to cut into portions. Serve hot.

# Meatloaf

This recipe is good for four hungry people. If there is any left over, eat it cold the next day. It is not a conventional meatloaf recipe as it contains carrot which adds a subtle taste sensation. You can prepare and cook it at home, or at camp you can use a Dutch oven, a loaf pan, or fashion a foil container. The only preparation needed is chopping the vegetables and mixing the ingredients to form the loaf.

Serves 4 Prep. time 5 mins Cooking time: about 1 hour

| | |
|---|---|
| **450 g** | **ground beef** |
| **2** | **large carrots, shredded** |
| **1** | **large onion, chopped** |
| **1** | **green pepper, diced, optional** |
| **1 cup/90 g** | **porridge oats** |
| **1** | **egg or egg powder equivalent** |
| **1 cup/240 ml** | **milk or reconstituted powdered milk** |
| **1 tsp** | **Worcestershire sauce** |
| | **salt and pepper, to taste** |

## At home:

Pre-heat the oven to 180°C/350°F. Mix all the ingredients in a large bowl until well blended. Place in a greased 23 x 12-cm loaf pan and cook in a pre-heated oven for 1 hour. The loaf should be firm on the outside and moist on the inside and the meat thoroughly cooked. Remove from the heat, pour off any fat and allow to cool completely. Wrap in plastic and then foil and refrigerate until needed.

## Or at camp:

Pre-heat a Dutch oven and place a sheet of greased foil on the bottom.
Place all the ingredients into a large bowl, mix thoroughly and form into a loaf shape.
Place the loaf on the foil and cook for 1 hour.
Remove, allow to cool and carve.
Serve sliced with your choice of side dishes.

# Lemon couscous with chicken

This is a very quick and easy meal to prepare because the couscous cooks faster and bulks up better than rice. The lemon adds a refreshing zing.

Serves **2** Prep. time: **5** mins Cooking time: **15–20** mins

| | |
|---|---|
| **900 g** | **chicken chunks** |
| **4** | **chicken bouillon cubes** |
| **pinch** | **lemon zest** |
| **1 cup/180 g** | **couscous** |
| **1 tbsp** | **oil** |
| **1 tsp** | **dried oregano** |
| **1 tsp** | **dried parsley** |
| | **salt and pepper, to taste** |

## At home:

To dehydrate the chicken, dice 900 g skinned chicken breasts to produce 225 g of dehydrated product (see p. 19). Pack in an airtight bag.

## At camp:

To rehydrate the chicken, add 2 cups/480 ml water and leave it to reconstitute in a sealed plastic bag. If you plan to eat the chicken for dinner, add the water earlier in the day
(at the lunch stop).

Fill a large pan with 3 cups/720 ml water and bring to the boil. Add the bouillon cubes, chicken and lemon zest and stir. Add the couscous and then immediately remove from the heat. Let the pan stand covered for about 5 minutes.

Fluff up the couscous with a fork and at the same time stir in the oil, oregano and parsley and season to taste. Serve hot.

# Fish in foil

This is a fast and delicious way to prepare fish whether you have caught it yourself or bought it locally. The recipe works for almost any kind of fish. You can prepare it in a Dutch oven or on the grill.

Serves 4 Prep. time: 10 mins Cooking time: 10–15 mins

| | |
|---|---|
| **2** | **fresh fish (cleaned to produce 4 fillets)** |
| **2** | **fresh jalapeno peppers** |
| **2 tbsp** | **oil** |
| **1 tsp** | **salt** |
| **2** | **cloves garlic, crushed** |
| **2 tsp** | **black pepper** |
| **2** | **lemons, cut into 8 segments** |

## At camp:

Pre-heat the Dutch oven or grill.

Place each fillet on its own square of aluminium foil.

Prepare the jalapenos by cutting off the top and, using a thin-bladed knife, dislodge and discard the seeds (the seeds are intensely hot). Slice the peppers thinly. Don't touch your eyes while working with peppers and wash your hands as soon as you have finished.

Brush the fillets with oil, season with salt, garlic and pepper. Arrange the jalapeno slices and squeeze the juice of 2 segments of lemon on top of each fillet. Fold the foil into a package, ensuring the sides are sealed. Bake in the oven or over the grill for 10 to 15 minutes (large fillets will take 5 to 10 minutes longer to cook). The fish is cooked when it flakes away easily with a fork. Serve hot.

# Ginger beef

You can enjoy a taste of the East with this grilled dish. Hoisin sauce is made from fermented soy beans, sugar, garlic and vinegar and is both sweet and spicy, and delicious basted onto barbecue ribs, chicken or, in this case, beef. It is available from Asian shops.

Serves 6 Prep. time: 25 mins Cooking time: 15 mins

| | |
|---|---|
| **1/2 cup/120 ml** | **hoisin sauce** |
| **1/2 cup/120 ml** | **sherry** |
| **1/2 cup/120 ml** | **soy sauce** |
| **4** | **spring onions, finely chopped** |
| **4** | **cloves garlic, crushed** |
| **2 tbsp** | **ground ginger** |
| **6 x 220-g** | **steaks** |

## At camp:

Mix the hoisin sauce, sherry, soy sauce, spring onions, garlic and ginger together in a large, sealable plastic bag.

Cut the steak across the grain into thick slices, about 5 cm thick.

Put the steak into the bag with the sauce, shake well and allow to marinate for up to 4 hours.

Fire up the grill, push the steak onto skewers and cook to your liking – about 2 minutes each side for medium rare, 3 minutes each side for medium to well done.

# Hungry hiker parcels

Serves 4 hungry hikers   Prep. time: 10 mins   Cooking time: 30 mins

| | |
|---|---|
| **450 g** | **ground beef** |
| **1** | **potato, peeled and cut into small cubes** |
| **1** | **carrot, peeled and cut into small strips** |
| **1** | **onion, finely chopped** |
| **4 tbsp** | **ketchup or tomato paste** |
| | **salt and pepper, to taste** |

## At camp:

Divide the meat into four portions and shape into patties. Mix and divide the prepared vegetables into four portions.

For each patty, take a square of foil and spread 1 tbsp of ketchup or tomato paste, mixed with a little water, in the centre. Place a meat patty on top of the ketchup, and then one portion of the mixed vegetables on top of the patty. Season to taste.

Fold the foil to form four parcels, sealing their tops and sides. Cook in hot embers for about 30 minutes. Serve piping hot.

# Sausage risotto

This version of risotto is the perfect one-pot meal. It has to take 30 minutes of your attention, so if you are starving it's not the best choice, unless you can provide some nibbles to eat while the dish is cooking. It is good with chicken or even fish flakes instead of the sausage – and even tastes good without any meat at all.

Serves 6 Prep. time: 10 mins Cooking time: 20–30 mins

| | |
|---|---|
| **1 tbsp** | **oil** |
| **2** | **cloves garlic, crushed** |
| **1** | **onion, finely chopped** |
| **570 g** | **long grain rice** |
| **4 cups/960 ml** | **hot chicken stock** |
| **1 cup/240 ml** | **canned chopped tomatoes, drained** |
| **1/2 cup/70 g** | **sliced mushrooms** |
| **2** | **large Italian salami sausage (about 110 g each), casings removed and sliced** |
| **1 tbsp** | **dried parsley** |

### At camp:

Heat the oil in a pan over medium heat and add the garlic and onion. Sauté until golden. Add the rice and stir it around to coat the grains.

Add 3 cups/720 ml of hot chicken stock and allow the liquid to simmer until the rice is soft to bite and is fluffy (about 15 to 20 minutes). Add the remaining stock, stirring occasionally, until absorbed by the rice.

Add the tomatoes, mushrooms and sausage and simmer until all the ingredients are hot. Just before removing from the heat, mix in the parsley.

# Ham and cheese potato stew

This is a great recipe for when you want something hot, filling and you want it fast. You can rustle up this dish in a Dutch oven, in a pan on the camp stove or you can prepare it in advance at home.

Serves 4 Prep. time: 5 mins Cooking time: 20 mins

| | |
|---|---|
| **2 tbsp** | **margarine** |
| **1** | **onion, finely chopped** |
| **1½ tbsp** | **plain flour** |
| **1 cup/240 ml** | **milk or reconstituted powdered milk** |
| | **salt and pepper, to taste** |
| **250 g** | **diced cooked ham** |
| **2** | **potatoes, thinly sliced** |
| **½ cup** | **grated cheddar cheese** |
| **1 tbsp** | **breadcrumbs** |

## At home:

Preheat the oven to 200ºC/400ºF. Melt the margarine in a small pan and sauté the onion for about 1 minute. Slowly add the flour, stirring continuously, to form a paste. Gradually add the milk until the sauce thickens. Season to taste.

Place the ham and potatoes in a casserole dish and add the sauce.

Cook for 15 minutes, remove, sprinkle the cheese and breadcrumbs over the top and cook for a further 5 minutes. Remove and allow to cool. Pack in an airtight bag. Refrigerate until you are leaving and use within two days.

## Or at camp:

Line a Dutch oven with foil or grease a large cooking pot and layer with the ham and potato.

Make the sauce as above and pour it over the layers of ham and potato.

Cook over a medium heat for 15 to 20 minutes Sprinkle the grated cheese and breadcrumbs over the top and cook for a few more minutes until the cheese has melted. Ladle out to serve.

# Curry couscous

Couscous is the camper's friend because it cooks faster than rice, bulks up better and imparts an interesting texture and flavour.

Serves **4** Prep. time: **5** mins Cooking time: **10** mins

| | |
|---|---|
| **1 cup** | **mixed vegetables (such as peas, carrots and beans)** |
| **1 tsp** | **curry powder** |
| **1** | **beef stock cube** |
| **1 tbsp** | **oil** |
| **1 cup/180 g** | **couscous** |

## At home:

Prepare the dehydrated vegetables (p. 19).

## At camp:

Fill a medium-sized pan with $1\frac{1}{2}$ cups/360 ml water. Add the vegetables, curry powder, crumbled beef stock cube and oil and bring to the boil.

Once the mixture has reached the boil, add the couscous and mix well. Immediately remove from the heat, cover and stand for 5 to 10 minutes until the couscous has softened. Serve hot.

# Corn fritters

You can prepare all the dry ingredients for this dish at home and pack them in one bag for convenience. These fritters are great with the chicken and apple stew (p. 95) and meatloaf (p. 100).

Serves 4 Prep. time: 7 mins Cooking time: 4–5 mins

| | |
|---|---|
| **120 ml** | **milk or reconstituted powdered milk** |
| **1 tbsp** | **egg powder** |
| **1/2 tsp** | **salt** |
| **1 1/2 tsp** | **baking powder** |
| **120 g** | **plain flour** |
| **150 g** | **dried or freeze-dried corn** |
| **1 tbsp** | **oil** |
| | **pepper, to taste** |

## At home:

Combine all the ingredients except the corn and oil, mix thoroughly and pack in one sealable plastic bag or container.

## At camp:

Soak the corn in 475 ml warm water for 5 minutes, then drain.

Add the corn to the dry ingredients and blend well. Add a little water, 1 teaspoon at a time, until the mixture forms a thick paste.

Heat the oil in a skillet over a hot flame and drop heaped tablespoons of fritter mix onto the pan. Reduce the heat and cook for 2 to 3 minutes until the bottom of the fritter is brown. Flip and cook the other side for 1 to 2 minutes. Serve immediately.

# Mexican rice

The diverse ingredients make this an out-of-the-ordinary side dish. You can also double the ingredients and prepare it as a main dinner dish. Eat with Lentil chilli (p. 94), Fish in foil (p. 102) or Meatloaf (p. 100).

Serves 2   Prep. time: 10 mins   Cooking time: 10 mins

| | |
|---|---|
| **1 cup/190 g** | **rice** |
| **1/2 cup** | **corn** |
| **1 tbsp** | **sliced onions** |
| **1 tbsp** | **sliced black olives** |
| **1/4 cup** | **chopped tomatoes** |
| **1/4 cup** | **diced red pepper** |
| **2 tbsp** | **chilli powder** |
| | **salt and pepper, to taste** |
| | **grated cheese, optional** |

## At home:

When dehydrating vegetables at home, do large batches at a time and take what you need for each recipe's requirements. For this recipe you can pack all the dried vegetables together in an airtight bag.

## At camp:

In a pan, boil 1 cup/240 ml salted water and add the rice. Cover and simmer for 15 minutes until all the liquid is absorbed and the rice is soft and fluffy. Set aside to keep warm.

In another pan, boil 1 cup/240 ml water and add the corn, onions, olives, tomatoes and peppers. Add the chilli powder to the vegetables and season to taste. The mixture should be moist but not runny. Stir the rice into the vegetable mixture and serve hot.

If you wish to use this recipe as a base for a one-pot rice dish and add pieces of beef or turkey, or beans, simply allow the additions to heat through.

Sprinkle a little grated cheese on top before serving.

# Scalloped potatoes

This is a convenient way to have potatoes available for any meal on the route because you can pack everything you need in one bag to make this delicious side dish.

Each bag serves 4 Prep. time: 10 mins plus dehydrating
Cooking time: 20 mins at home, 20 mins at the campsite

| | |
|---|---|
| **1.8 kg** | **potatoes** |
| **2 cups/140 g** | **powdered milk** |
| **1 cup** | **grated Parmesan** |
| **2** | **onions, sliced** |
| **1/2 cup** | **bacon bits** |
| **1/2 cup** | **plain flour** |
| **1/2 cup** | **coffee creamer powder** |
| | **salt and pepper, to taste** |

## At home:

Peel the potatoes and boil them for 20 minutes. Drain and allow to cool.

Cut the potatoes into 5-mm thick slices, place on a large baking tray and dehydrate in the oven at about 56°C/130°F for 5 to 6 hours.

When dried, divide into four separate bags and add to each bag: a quarter of the powdered milk, Parmesan, onion slices, bacon bits, flour, creamer. Season to taste. Seal.

## At camp:

To rehydrate the bags, add enough water to cover the contents and let stand to rehydrate for 1 hour.

When reconstituted, place the contents of the bags in a pan and bring to the boil. Cover and simmer until the potatoes thicken up. Remove from the heat and let stand for 5 to 10 minutes. Fluff up with a fork and serve hot.

# Potatoes and green beans

While you can dehydrate all the vegetables for this side dish before you set off, then rehydrate for 30 to 45 minutes, fresh ingredients are recommended. Either way, it is a simple and nourishing vegetable combination.

Serves 4 Prep. time: 5 mins Cooking time: 5–10 mins

| | |
|---|---|
| **3** | **medium potatoes, boiled and sliced** |
| **1/2 cup** | **cooked green beans or 250 g fresh green beans** |
| **1** | **onion, sliced** |
| **110-g** | **packet onion instant soup powder** |

## At camp:

Place the vegetables in the centre of a piece of foil and sprinkle over the onion soup powder. Fold the foil into a sealed parcel and place close to the fire or stove until all the ingredients are heated and cooked through.

# Carrot and cabbage salad

This is an unusual combination for a salad but it works well, especially as a side dish with Sausage risotto (p. 105), or for lunch.

Serves 4 Prep. time: 5 mins

| | |
|---|---|
| **1/2 cup** | **shredded cabbage** |
| **1/2 cup** | **shredded carrots** |
| **pinch** | **celery salt** |
| **1/4 cup/80 g** | **raisins** |
| **1 tbsp** | **oil** |
| **1 tbsp** | **red wine vinegar** |

## At home:

Shred the cabbage and carrots and dehydrate in the oven (see page 19).
To produce 1/2 cup you will need to use at least 450 g of fresh produce.
Store in airtight bags.

## At camp:

Rehydrate the cabbage and carrot in 1 1/2 cups/360 ml water for 20 to 25 minutes.
Drain and add the celery salt.
Stir in the raisins, oil and vinegar and mix well. Serve cold.

# Camp coleslaw

This is a quick and refreshing side dish whether it's hot or cold. You can use dehydrated cabbage and onion and combine them at home to save time.

Serves 4 to 6   Prep. time: 10 mins

| | |
|---|---|
| ⚙ **1** | **medium-sized cabbage, shredded finely** |
| **1/2** | **cucumber, peeled and finely chopped** |
| ⚙ **1** | **onion, sliced** |
| **1 tbsp** | **raisins (optional – but worth it)** |
| | **salt to taste** |
| **1 cup/240 ml** | **mayonnaise** |
| **1/4 cup** | **unsweetened orange juice** |

## At home:

Finely shred the cabbage, spread on a large baking sheet and dehydrate in the oven at around 55°C/130°F for 5 to 6 hours.

## At camp:

Reconstitute the cabbage by placing in a bowl and covering with water. Add additional water as necessary until the cabbage is fully reconstituted, then drain.

Mix the cabbage, cucumber, onion, raisins and salt together in a bowl. Blend the mayonnaise and orange juice together and pour it over the cabbage mixture. Toss thoroughly to coat the vegetables. Serve cold.

# Breads & cakes

Bread is one the great camping foods because it is so versatile. It complements any meal. Crispy bread and rye bread will last for several days. When it is getting stale, you can break it up and add it to stews and other dishes. Many of the bread recipes that follow can be made either at home or at camp – so enjoy.

# Trail bread

Just the smell of bread cooking on camp makes the effort worthwhile. This recipe was developed by American settlers as they moved west on the wagon trains. It couldn't be easier now with the use of a Dutch oven. If you prefer to make it ahead at home, it freezes well too. On the path it will keep for three or four days and longer in cool weather. It is a versatile recipe: use more honey by reducing the equivalent amount of water or sprinkle in sultanas or add thinly sliced salami.

Makes 2 loaves (30–36 slices) Prep. time: 5 mins Cooking time: 45 mins

| | |
|---|---|
| **1/3 cup** | **honey** |
| **2 1/2 tbsp** | **active dry yeast** |
| **3 cups/720 ml** | **warm water** |
| **2 tbsp** | **vegetable oil** |
| **2 tbsp** | **salt** |
| **1.2 kg** | **bread flour** |

## At camp:

In a large bowl, dissolve the honey and yeast in the warm water and let stand for about 10 minutes.

Stir in the oil, salt and 4 cups (480 g) of the flour. Gradually blend in the remaining flour until you have a firm dough. Remove from the bowl and, on a lightly floured baking mat, knead for 10 to 15 minutes until soft. The dough should not stick to your hands. Place in a lightly oiled bowl, cover and allow to rise for about 1 hour. The dough needs to be warm so stand it near the fire or stove if the air is cool.

Divide the dough into two equal pieces and shape into loaves. Place in two lightly greased 23 x 12-cm loaf pans. Cover the pans with a damp cloth, and allow to rise for another 35 to 40 minutes until they have doubled in volume.

While this is happening, pre-heat a Dutch oven to a medium-hot temperature.

Bake the loaves for 45 to 60 minutes. The loaves are ready when they give a hollow sound when tapped on the bottom.

(If you bake this at home the oven temperature should be 190°C/375°F.)

Serve warm with lots of butter or honey.

# Indian fry bread

Also known as Navajo Taco, this bread has been made by Native Americans for centuries. It's enjoyed with savoury or sweet fillings or rolled in sugar for a dessert.

Makes **24** rounds Prep. time: **25** mins Cooking time: **2–3** mins each

| | |
|---|---|
| **2 cups/240 g** | **plain flour** |
| **2 tsp** | **baking powder** |
| **1/4 cup** | **sugar, optional** |
| **1/2 cup** | **powdered milk** |
| **pinch** | **salt** |
| **1 cup/240 ml** | **warm water** |
| | **vegetable oil, for deep-frying** |

## At camp:

Mix the flour, baking powder, sugar, powdered milk and salt together in a large bowl. Stir in the warm (not hot) water and mix with a fork and your hands to produce a soft dough. Let stand for 30 minutes to rise.

Pull off pieces of the dough and fashion into rounds about golf-ball size, and flatten. Add oil to a skillet to a depth of 2.5 cm and heat to 180°C/350°F. Test whether it is the right temperature by dropping a piece of dough into the oil – if it sizzles immediately, the oil is hot enough. Deep-fry 3 or 4 dough rounds at a time for 1 to 2 minutes, until they are golden brown. Remove, drain and serve piping hot.

Serve with a savoury filling such as cheese or cooked meats. Fold over to make a taco. Alternatively, serve with sweet fillings such as sugar, honey, maple syrup or berries, or roll them in cinnamon and sugar.

## Trailside tip:

- Pack an 'S'-shaped hook: one end fits over a makeshift tripod and the pot is suspended from the other end by its handle. If there's enough wood to light a fire, there is enough to fashion a few basic utensils, such as skewers or a spit.

# Bannock

Bannock bread originated in Scotland and Ireland centuries ago. Emigrants have carried the recipe around the world and adapted it. Traditionally it is a flat, unleavened bread made of oatmeal or barley flour and is usually cooked on a griddle or on hot stones. Fresh blueberries make an excellent addition to this bread. Because it is easy to make and uses so few ingredients it has long been a favourite with travellers and variations of it are found worldwide.

Makes 1 x 1 lb/450 g cake    Prep. time: 10 mins
Cooking time: 10–15 mins

| | |
|---|---|
| **4 cups/480 g** | **plain or potato flour** |
| **2½ tbsp** | **baking powder** |
| **1 tsp** | **salt** |
| **1 tsp** | **sugar** |
| | **knob of butter** |

## At camp:

Mix the flour, baking powder, salt and sugar thoroughly. Gradually stir in enough water to make a thick, smooth batter, about the consistency of single cream.

Heat a knob of butter in a large skillet and pour in enough batter to a depth of about 2.5 cm. Place the skillet on hot coals.

Cook for 5 to 7 minutes and then flip the bread over to cook the other side for 5 to 7 minutes, until golden brown. Check the bannock is cooked all the way through by poking a skewer in the centre. If no dough sticks it is cooked.

To serve, tear the bannock apart rather than cutting it with a knife, and spread with honey or butter and devour.

# Damper bread

This is a traditional Australian bread that can be cooked in a Dutch oven, but is best baked on the hot coals of a campfire.

Makes **1** large loaf Prep. time: **10** mins Cooking time: **30** mins

| | |
|---|---|
| **4 cups/480 g** | **plain flour** |
| **1/2 tsp** | **salt** |
| **2 tbsp** | **butter** |
| **1 1/2 cups/360 ml** | **milk or reconstituted powdered milk** |

## At camp:

Mix the flour and salt in a large bowl. Rub in the butter with your hands until you have a breadcrumb-like texture. Make a well in the centre and slowly pour in the milk, stirring to combine until you have a firm dough.

Place the dough on a floured baking mat and knead into a round shape.

Place on a greased baking sheet or sheet of foil and, using a knife, make a crisscross in the top the dough. Bake in a Dutch oven sitting in hot ashes of a campfire for about 30 minutes, until golden brown. Alternatively, you can place the dough on a griddle directly on top of the hot embers. Serve warm with butter and honey.

# Pancakes

This is a favourite in North America, and tastes best when served around the campfire in a skillet or on the griddle. The dry ingredients can be batched together at home.

Makes 12 Prep. time: 10 mins Cooking time: 3 mins

| | |
|---|---|
| **3 cups/360 g** | **plain flour** |
| **1 cup/160 g** | **cornmeal** |
| **2 tbsp** | **baking powder** |
| **3 tbsp** | **sugar** |
| **1 tsp** | **salt** |
| **4** | **eggs or egg powder equivalent** |
| | **vegetable oil** |
| **3 cups/720 ml** | **milk** |
| **2 drops** | **vanilla extract** |

## At camp:

In a large bowl, mix together the flour, cornmeal, baking powder, sugar and salt.
Beat the eggs and blend them into the flour mixture, along with 40 ml of the oil, the milk and vanilla. Whip with a fork until you have a thin batter.
Allow the batter to rest for a few minutes and it will start to thicken.
Heat a skillet and add 1 tbsp of oil. Pour in enough batter, about 2 tbsp, to make a pancake about 15 cm in diameter. Cook for 1 to 2 minutes. Flip the pancake and cook for a further minute or so, until golden brown.
Serve with jam, fruit, honey, lemon juice and sugar.

# Honey doughnuts

Camp honey doughnuts are easy and quick to make and delicious to eat when fresh and hot. The key to good doughnuts is the oil temperature – it must be right for the doughnuts to expand and cook properly. If it is too cold, they will turn out too oily; if it is too hot they will burn, so experiment by dropping small pieces of doughnuts in the oil. Once the mixture swells up right away, the temperature is spot on.

Makes 12 Prep. time: 15 mins Standing time: 3 hours
Cooking time: Seconds!

| | |
|---|---|
| **1 tbsp** | **active dry yeast** |
| **1/2 cup/120 ml** | **warm water** |
| **1** | **egg or egg powder equivalent** |
| **1/2 tsp** | **salt** |
| **1 tbsp** | **vegetable oil plus extra for deep-frying** |
| **3 cups/360 g** | **plain flour** |
| **1 tsp** | **sugar** |
| | **honey, to taste** |
| | **cinnamon, to taste** |

## At camp:

In a large bowl, mix together the yeast with the warm water. Add the egg, salt, 1 tbsp of oil, flour and sugar, and mix until you have a firm dough.

Knead the dough on a floured board or surface for 4 or 5 minutes. Leave in a warm place for about 2 hours until the dough has doubled in size.

Roll flat and cut into 4 cm squares and leave for a further hour to rise.

When you are ready to deep-fry, pour the oil into a large skillet to a depth of 4 to 5 cm, and heat. Drop in balls of dough, two or three at a time.

Cook for just seconds and remove the doughnuts when they are golden brown

Drain and serve hot, dipped in honey and sprinkled with cinnamon.

# Banana bread

You can make this nutritious banana bread at home – it keeps well on the hike – or you bake it at the campsite in a Dutch oven.

Makes 1 x 1 lb/450 g loaf Prep. time: 10 mins
Cooking time: 50–60 mins

| | |
|---|---|
| **3/4 cup/225 g** | **honey** |
| **1/4 cup** | **butter or oil** |
| **2** | **eggs or egg powder equivalent** |
| **4** | **bananas** |
| **1/2 cup/120 ml** | **buttermilk** |
| **1 tsp** | **vanilla extract** |
| **2 1/2 cups/300 g** | **plain flour** |
| **1 tsp** | **bicarbonate of soda** |
| **1 tsp** | **salt** |
| **1 cup/150 g** | **chopped nuts** |
| **1/2 cup/110 g** | **chocolate chips** |

## At home:

Preheat the oven to 180°C/350°F. Grease a 23 x 12-cm bread pan.

Mix the honey and butter in large bowl, and blend in the eggs. Mash the bananas and add them, with the buttermilk and vanilla, to the mixture. Beat until smooth.

Fold in the flour, bicarbonate of soda and salt, and stir in the nuts and chocolate chips.

Spoon the mixture into the bread pan and bake for 1 hour. Test to see if it is ready by sticking a skewer into the centre. If it comes out clean, it is cooked.

Remove from the pan and allow to cool. Pack in foil – it will keep for several days.

## At camp:

Line the base and sides of a Dutch oven with foil.

Follow the directions above to prepare the mixture and spoon it directly onto the foil.

Pile a layer of embers on the lid so that the mixture cooks from top and bottom. Bake for 1 hour. Test as above. Remove from the oven by taking hold of both sides of the foil and lifting the bread out. Allow to cool, before serving.

# Chocolate muffins

You can bake these muffins at home and freeze until needed or make them in a Dutch oven while out camping. If you make them at home, thaw them the day before you leave and they will keep for about a week under most conditions.

Makes 12 Prep. time: 10 mins Cooking time: 15–20 mins

| | |
|---|---|
| **3** | **eggs or egg powder equivalent** |
| **1 1/2 cups/300 g** | **sugar** |
| **2/3 cup** | **oil** |
| **1/3 cup** | **puréed apple sauce** |
| **1 tbsp** | **vanilla extract** |
| **1 cup/150 g** | **chopped walnuts** |
| **1 cup/225 g** | **chocolate chips** |
| **2 1/2 cups/300 g** | **plain flour** |
| **1 tsp** | **baking powder** |
| **1 tsp** | **bicarbonate of soda** |
| **1/2 tsp** | **salt** |
| **1 tbsp** | **cinnamon, optional** |
| **1/2 cup/120 g** | **powdered drinking chocolate** |

## At home:

Preheat the oven to 190ºC/375ºF. With a fork or whisk, mix together the eggs, sugar, oil, apple sauce, vanilla, nuts and chocolate chips. Sift in and blend the flour, baking powder, bicarbonate of soda, salt, cinnamon and powdered chocolate.

Spoon the mixture into a 12-cup muffin pan and bake for 15 to 20 minutes or until golden brown.

Pack in airtight bags and freeze until needed.

## Or at camp:

Pre-heat the Dutch oven over the fire embers.

Prepare the mixture as above and spoon into a round muffin pan. Bake in the Dutch oven for 20 to 30 minutes or until golden brown.

# Weekend gourmet

Camping and feasting – there are few things better than dining out under the stars with fine wine, good food and best friends.

The following recipes will allow you to dine out in style – to enjoy the ambience of eating *al fresco*. The meals are not intended for the lightweight camper although some can certainly be created on a couple of camping stoves. Instead, we have assumed that you are able to transport in all the items you will need to enjoy a gastronomic treat. So load up the tables, rugs, and the grill, and pack candles to add an extra touch of glamour.

# Chicken primavera

Primavera literally means 'spring style' in Italian and relies on young, fresh and tender vegetables to produce a light, flavourful garnish for the chicken. Follow this with the fruitiness of the Pineapple sundae, opposite, for a memorable dessert.

Serves 8 Prep. time: 15 mins Cooking time: 20 mins

| | |
|---|---|
| **2 tbsp** | **oil** |
| **900 g** | **chicken breast, skinned and cut into bite-sized cubes** |
| **1/3 cup** | **cornflour** |
| **4 cups/960 ml** | **chicken stock** |
| **1** | **head broccoli florets** |
| **1** | **green pepper, diced** |
| **1** | **red pepper, diced** |
| **2** | **carrots, finely sliced** |
| **2** | **onions, finely sliced** |
| **450 g** | **spaghetti** |
| **2 tbsp** | **grated Parmesan** |
| | **salt and pepper, to taste** |

## At camp:

In a skillet, heat the oil and sauté the chicken until golden brown and cooked through, about 10 minutes. Remove from the heat and keep warm.

Blend the cornflour with 1/2 cup/120 ml of the stock to make a smooth paste. Pour the remainder of the stock into a large pan. Set over a medium heat and add the broccoli, peppers, carrot and onion and bring to the boil. Reduce the heat to low and cook until the vegetables are tender, 7 to 10 minutes.

Add the cornflour paste and stir continuously until the mixture boils and thickens. Add the chicken and heat through.

In a separate pan, bring salted water to the boil and cook the spaghetti on a rolling boil until *al dente*, 8 to 10 minutes. Drain.

Serve the spaghetti in large bowls, topped with the chicken and vegetables. Finish with a sprinkling of grated Parmesan, and season to taste.

# Pineapple sundae

Serves 8 Prep. time: 10 mins

| | |
|---|---|
| **2** | **fresh pineapples, cut into chunks** |
| **300 g** | **sweet orange segments** |
| **2** | **bananas, cut into chunks** |
| **4 tbsp** | **finely chopped crystallised ginger** |
| **4 cups/960 ml** | **natural yoghurt** |
| **2 tsp** | **vanilla extract** |
| **2 tsp** | **sugar** |

## At camp:

Mix the pineapple, orange, banana and most of the ginger together in one bowl.
In a separate bowl, mix the yoghurt, vanilla and sugar.
Into glasses or colourful transparent picnic ware, layer alternately the fruit and yoghurt mix. Sprinkle the remaining chopped ginger on top to serve.

# Floridian lamb kebabs

Delicious lamb kebabs are great for a party. We call this Floridian lamb because, while you will rarely see sheep in the Sunshine State, we do have a lot of orange trees. Make up the marinade the day before, add the lamb and by the time you come to grill it, all the flavours will be absorbed. Follow with Just peachy, a subtle, rum-infused dessert.

Serves 8   Prep. time: 20 mins   Cooking time: 30 mins

| | |
|---|---|
| **1.2 kg** | **boned lamb, cubed** |
| **3 tbsp** | **ground coriander** |
| **4 cups/960 ml** | **fresh orange juice** |
| **2/3 cup** | **orange liqueur, optional** |
| **1** | **jalapeno pepper, seeds removed and cut into tiny pieces** |
| **6** | **oranges, peeled, pips removed and cut into slices** |

## At home:

Rub the ground coriander into the cubed meat.

In a large bowl, mix the meat with the orange juice, liqueur and pepper. Cover and marinate in the fridge overnight.

Before leaving home, transfer the meat and marinade into a large plastic container. Keep cool.

## At camp:

Fire up the grill to a medium heat. Put out two bowls, one for the meat and the other for the orange slices.

Pour the marinade into a small pan, bring to the boil and simmer, uncovered, until it has reduced to a sticky orange sauce. Set aside.

Take a skewer and thread a piece of lamb, then a slice of orange and repeat until the skewer is full. Repeat with the other skewers. Place the skewers on the grill and cook to your liking.

Remove the meat and orange slices from the skewers, arrange on plates and drizzle with the sauce. Serve with Scalloped potatoes (p. 110) and maybe a green salad.

# Just peachy

Serves 8 Prep. time: 20 mins

| | |
|---|---|
| **1.8 kg** | **fresh peaches, peeled, stoned and sliced** |
| **1 1/2 tsp** | **ground ginger** |
| **1 1/3 cups/320 ml** | **double cream** |
| **2 tbsp** | **rum** |

## At home:

Purée the peaches and ginger and pack into an airtight container. Keep chilled.

## At camp:

Empty the peach purée into a large bowl, stir in the double cream and rum. Serve in pretty glasses or bowls.

# Goulash

Start with this classic dish that can be prepared quickly if necessary or simmered gently for even richer flavours, leaving you free to mingle with your friends. Follow by serving Fruit grill, opposite, a decadent dessert that can involve everyone in the cooking.

Serves 8 Prep. time: 10 mins
Cooking time: 20–30 mins (but will happily simmer far longer)

| | |
|---|---|
| **2 tbsp** | **oil** |
| **900 g** | **lean beef, cubed** |
| **2** | **onions, finely chopped** |
| **2 x 450-g** | **cans chopped tomatoes** |
| **1** | **green pepper, diced** |
| **1** | **stick celery, chopped** |
| **2 tbsp** | **paprika** |
| **1 tsp** | **dried basil** |
| **1 tsp** | **marjoram** |
| | **salt and pepper, to taste** |
| **1 cup/240 ml** | **sour cream** |
| **3 cups/170 g** | **medium dried egg noodles** |
| **bunch** | **parsley, chopped** |

## At camp:

Heat the oil in a large pan. Sear the meat in the hot oil until browned on all sides. Remove and set aside.

Sauté the onions for 5 minutes, until softened. Add the tomatoes, pepper, celery, paprika, basil, marjoram and season to taste.

Return the meat to the skillet, add the soured cream and stir well to combine all the ingredients. Cover the pan and simmer gently for 30 minutes, stirring occasionally.

Approximately 10 minutes before you are ready to serve the goulash, bring a pan of salted water to the boil and plunge the noodles in to cook on a rolling boil for 5 to 8 minutes. Drain thoroughly.

Serve the noodles topped with spoonfuls of rich goulash. Sprinkle chopped parsley over the top for a gourmet finish.

# Fruit grill

Serves 8 Prep. time: 5 mins Cooking time: 15 mins

| | |
|---|---|
| **2.4 kg** | **assorted fresh chopped fruits (such as cherries, bananas, apricots, plums, strawberries, pineapple and peaches)** |
| **30** | **marshmallows** |
| **1 cup/225 g** | **chocolate chips** |
| | **cream or natural yoghurt, to serve** |

## At camp:

Lightly grease a 35 x 23-cm baking sheet. Spread the chopped fruit evenly over the sheet and distribute the marshmallows on top. The aim is to try to cover all the fruit with the marshmallows so that when they melt they form a layer above the fruit. Sprinkle the chocolate chips on top of the marshmallows.

Cover the sheet with foil, making sure all sides are sealed. Then rest the baking sheet on the grill for 10 to 15 minutes, to melt the marshmallows and chocolate.

Remove from heat and carefully remove the foil. Allow to cool for about 3 minutes. Slice and serve with cream or yoghurt.

# Vegetarian chilli

This chilli is not only healthy and wholesome, it is bursting with flavour as well. Follow it with Banana boats, opposite, with a dash of rum to keep out any late-evening chill. Although the dessert is best cooked in the embers of a fire, it can be cooked on a grill or stove. However you cook it, it is delicious.

Serves 6 Prep. time: 10 mins Cooking time: 30 mins

| | |
|---|---|
| **1½ cups/360 ml** | **vegetable stock** |
| **3** | **courgettes/zucchini, chopped** |
| **450-g** | **can chopped tomatoes** |
| **2** | **carrots, diced** |
| **1** | **green pepper, diced** |
| **1 tbsp** | **chilli powder** |
| **1 tsp** | **ground cumin** |
| **½ tsp** | **dried thyme** |
| **1½ cups/225 g** | **canned black beans, drained** |
| **1½ cups/340 g** | **canned chickpeas, drained** |
| **1 tbsp** | **oil** |
| **4 cups/750 g** | **long grain rice** |
| | **crème fraiche or sour cream, to serve** |

## At camp:

In a large pan, bring the stock to the boil over a medium heat and add the courgettes/zucchini, tomatoes, carrots, pepper, chilli powder, cumin and thyme. Return to the boil, cover and simmer gently for 20 minutes. Do not overcook the vegetables; they should be tender but not mushy.

Add the black beans and chickpeas and increase the temperature to heat through for a further 5 minutes.

In a separate large pan, heat the oil and shoot in the rice, stirring until the grains are coated. Add 2 litres of hot water and return to the boil. Stir once and cover. Reduce the heat and simmer for 15 minutes until all the liquid is absorbed.

Serve with some soured cream and a side of Tomato, cucumber and red onion salad (p. 82).

# Banana boats

Serves 6 Prep. time: 5 mins Cooking time: 5 mins

| | |
|---|---|
| **6** | **bananas** |
| **6 tbsp** | **chocolate chips** |
| **4 tbsp** | **brown sugar** |
| **2 tbsp** | **rum or cognac** |

## At camp:

Peel back one flap on each banana so that the whole of one side is exposed. Make sure the flap is still attached at one end. Make a slit lengthways down the banana being careful not to cut all the way through. Then gently lever the cut apart to make a cavity.

In this slit, sprinkle chocolate chips, top with brown sugar and drizzle over 1 tsp rum or cognac. Repeat with the other bananas.

Replace the flap of peel and individually wrap the bananas tightly in foil. Place in the embers of a fire for about 5 minutes, or until the chocolate and sugar have melted. Pull away the foil and use this as dishes to serve.

# Almond chicken

A great summer evening's dinner combination – both this Almond chicken recipe and the Zabaglione, opposite, are packed with flavour, but neither is very heavy so you could even go for a starlight stroll or a midnight swim after the meal.

Serves 4 Prep. time: 10 mins Cooking time: 20 mins

| | |
|---|---|
| **1 tbsp** | **oil** |
| **2** | **large chicken breasts and diced** |
| **1** | **onion, finely chopped** |
| **2** | **sticks celery, diced** |
| **1** | **carrot, thinly sliced** |
| **1/2 cup/40 g** | **almonds, finely chopped** |
| **2 tbsp** | **lemon juice** |
| **1 cup/240 ml** | **single cream** |
| | **salt and pepper, to taste** |
| **1/2 cup/75 g** | **croutons or cubes of crusty bread** |
| **1 cup/110 g** | **cheddar cheese, grated** |
| | **rice or noodles, to serve** |

## At camp:

Heat the oil in a large pan over hot embers, add the chicken and sauté for about 10 minutes until golden brown and cooked through. Remove from the pan and set aside to keep warm.

Add the onion, celery, carrot and almonds, and stir to make sure all the ingredients are coated with oil. Sauté gently until the vegetables are tender, 2 to 3 minutes. Return the chicken to the pan, along with the lemon juice and cream. Stir and season to taste. Sprinkle over the croutons and the cheese, and allow to heat through until the cheese melts. Serve on a bed of rice or with noodles.

# Zabaglione

Serves 4 Prep. time: 5 mins Cooking time: 15–20 mins

| | |
|---|---|
| **5** | **egg yolks** |
| **1/2 cup/100 g** | **sugar** |
| **1/2 cup/240 ml** | **Marsala wine** |

## At camp:

In a large pan, fill water to a depth of 6 cm and bring to the boil.

In a smaller pan that will sit inside the larger pan, combine the egg yolks and sugar until smooth. Add the Marsala and, stirring continuously, allow the mixture to heat through and thicken. Serve warm, as soon as it thickens, in glasses or bowls.

# Chicken chasseur

This chicken dish is both delicious and very filling and works well served with fresh crusty bread and a good French country wine. The dessert opposite is a fitting accompaniment as it is light and refreshing after such a hearty main course.

Serves 8 Prep. time: 10 mins Cooking time: 20–25 mins

| | |
|---|---|
| **2 tbsp** | **oil** |
| **8** | **chicken breasts, cut into thick strips** |
| | **salt and pepper, to taste** |
| **2 tbsp** | **butter** |
| **2** | **onions, finely chopped** |
| **3 cups/210 g** | **sliced mushrooms** |
| **6** | **cloves garlic, roughly chopped** |
| **1 tbsp** | **flour** |
| **1 cup/240 ml** | **chicken stock** |
| **1/2 cup/120 ml** | **red wine** |
| **4** | **large tomatoes, chopped** |
| **pinch** | **dried thyme** |
| | **fresh parsley, chopped** |
| | **mashed potatoes, to serve** |

## At camp:

Heat the oil in a skillet over a moderate heat and brown the chicken. Turn frequently to ensure thorough cooking and season. Remove the chicken from the pan and keep warm.

Add the butter to the pan and sauté the onion until golden. Add the mushrooms and garlic and sauté for 5 minutes. Stir the flour into the juices until blended and then add the stock, wine, tomatoes and thyme.

Return the chicken to the pan, cover and simmer for about 5 minutes, or until warmed through. Sprinkle over the parsley and season to taste. Serve with creamy mashed potatoes.

# Mint chocolate pots

Serves 8 Prep. time: 10 mins

| | |
|---|---|
| **3/4 cup/150 g** | **sugar** |
| **1/3 cup/75 g** | **unsweetened cocoa** |
| **1/4 cup/30 g** | **plain flour** |
| **2 1/3 cups/560 ml** | **milk** |
| **2** | **egg yolks** |
| **1 1/2 cups/110 g** | **mint chocolate chips** |
| **1 tsp** | **vanilla extract** |
| **1 tbsp** | **butter** |
| **2 cups/225 g** | **strawberries** |

## At home:

In a large pan, combine the sugar, cocoa and flour and slowly stir in the milk.

Cook over a medium heat, stirring frequently, until the mixture thickens and starts to bubble. Reduce the heat and cook for a further 2 minutes, then remove from heat.

Pour half the mixture into a bowl and beat in the egg yolks. When thoroughly blended, return the contents of the bowl to the pan.

Add the mint chocolate chips and bring back to a gentle bubbling boil, stirring frequently. Reduce the heat and simmer, stirring occasionally, for a further 2 minutes.

Stir in the vanilla and butter and simmer for 1 minute. Pour the mixture into a sealable container, leave to cool, cover and refrigerate.

Transport in a container and keep cool.

Serve with fresh strawberries with their hulls intact, so that they can be dipped into the chocolate.

# Jambalaya

Jambalaya is our family favourite and we have cooked it many times while camping out in the Ocala National Forest, one of the best places to spot Florida's dwindling population of black bears. Whether you cook it at home or at camp, it is always memorable. Experiment with the ingredients: add diced chicken breast and prawns to turn it into an even more sumptuous feast. Berries galore, opposite, to follow is a fruity and refreshing dessert.

Serves **8** Prep. time: **10** mins Cooking time: **10–15** mins

| | |
|---|---|
| **2 tbsp** | **oil** |
| **2** | **onions, finely chopped** |
| **8** | **cloves garlic, crushed** |
| **900 g** | **Italian sausages, sliced into chunks** |
| **3 cups/570 g** | **long grain rice** |
| **3 cups/720 ml** | **chicken stock** |
| **4** | **large tomatoes chopped** |
| **2** | **green peppers, sliced** |
| **1 tsp** | **ground cumin** |
| **1 tbsp** | **Tabasco** |
| | **salt and pepper, to taste** |

### At camp:

Heat the oil in a large skillet or wok over a moderate heat. Sauté the onions and garlic for about 2 minutes, until they are softened. Add the sausage and cook for a further minute. Stir in the rice, stock, tomatoes, pepper, cumin, Tabasco and seasoning. Combine well and bring to the boil. Cover and simmer for 10 to 15 minutes, stirring occasionally, until the rice is soft.

Remove from the heat and let stand, covered, until all the liquid has been absorbed. Fluff up with a fork before serving.

# Berries galore

Serves 8 Prep. time: 5 mins Cooking time: 10–15 mins

| | |
|---|---|
| **2 cups/380 g** | **wild or brown rice** |
| **4 cups/600 g** | **fresh berries (such as blackberries, blueberries, blackcurrants and raspberries)** |
| **2 cups/480 ml** | **water** |
| **1½ cups/300 g** | **sugar** |
| **½ tsp** | **salt** |
| **4 tsp** | **cornflour** |
| **2 tbsp** | **lemon juice** |
| | **single cream or yoghurt, to serve** |

## At camp:

Cook the rice in boiling water until soft. Remove from the heat and keep warm.

Put the whole berries, 1½ cups/360 ml of the water, the sugar and salt into a pan and stir over a gentle heat until the sugar is completely dissolved.

Blend the cornflour with the remaining ½ cup/120 ml of water to make a thin paste, and stir it into the fruit syrup. Warm over a medium heat until the sauce thickens and clears. Add the lemon juice and cooked rice and heat through.

Remove the mixture from heat and serve slightly warm in bowls, with thick yoghurt or single cream.

# Stuffed trout

If you are a successful angler you may be able to catch enough fish for this meal. If not, buy them. The basil and rosemary impart a wonderful flavour to the fish which should just fall off the bone when cooked over the fire. Follow very simply with fresh fruit and chocolate – everyone's desire.

Serves 8 Prep. time: 15 mins Cooking time: 15 mins

| | |
|---|---|
| **8** | **medium trout** |
| **8** | **cloves garlic, crushed** |
| **4** | **lemons, 3 halved and 1 cut into 8 slices** |
| **8** | **sprigs fresh basil** |
| **8** | **sprigs fresh rosemary** |
| | **salt and pepper, to taste** |

## At camp:

Fire up the grill to a medium-high heat.

Prepare the trout by cleaning and removing heads.

Stuff the inside cavity with 1 slice of lemon, 1 crushed clove garlic and a sprig each of basil and rosemary. Season with salt and pepper. Wrap each fish in foil and cook over direct heat for 15 to 18 minutes. Alternatively, fry the fish in a large skillet. It is cooked when it flakes easily.

Remove the sprigs before serving, and apportion each plate pieces of lemon to squeeze over the fish.

## Trailside tips:

- Save some lemon to rub on your hands after cooking and eating. The juice will remove any fishy smells.
- Don't be afraid to spice up your food, especially on a cold night, with plenty of garlic as well as paprika or cayenne pepper.

# Chocolate fondue

Serves 8 Prep. time: 5 mins Cooking time: 10 mins

| | |
|---|---|
| **3 cups/675 g** | **chocolate chips** |
| **1 cup/240 ml** | **milk** |
| **4 cups/600 g** | **fresh fruit (such as apples, bananas, pears, strawberries, cut into large chunks)** |

## At camp:

Melt the chocolate chips in a pan over a very low heat, taking care to ensure the mixture doesn't burn. Add the milk and stir continuously until the mixture starts to bubble gently.

Remove from the heat and serve immediately in the pot, placed in the centre of the group. Everyone dips chunks of fruit into the chocolate and if a piece of fruit is lost into the chocolate a forfeit has to be performed by the offender!

# Resources & Acknowledgements

## FURTHER READING


***Navigation and Bushcraft***

*Essential Bushcraft*, Mears, R., Coronet Books, 2003

*How to Shit in the Woods: An Environmentally Sound Approach to a Lost Art*, Meyer, K., Ten Speed Press, 1994

*Map and Compass: The Art of Navigation*, Hawkins, P., Cicerone Press, 2004

*Mountain Leadership Training Boards of Great Britain*, Langmuir, E., Scottish Council of Physical Recreation, 1969

*Tom Brown's Field Guide to Wilderness Survival*, Brown, T., Warner Books, 1989

***Nature Guides***

*Collins Field Guide: Bird Songs and Calls of Britain and Northern Europe*, Sample, G., Collins 1996

*Collins Nature Guide: Healing Plants of Britain and Europe*, Podlech, D., Collins, 1996

*Food for Free*, Mabey, R., Collins, 2001

*Guide to Wild Flowers of Britain and Europe*, Aichele, D., Hamlyn, 2001

*Identifying and Harvesting Edible and Medicinal Plants*, Brill, S., Quill, 1994

*Pick of the Bunch*, Johnson, P., Longacre Press 1997

*Tracking and the Art of Seeing*, Rezendes, P., HarperCollins, 1999


## CAMPING SUPPLIERS

The following are websites for suppliers of camping and outdoors equipment. Use these websites to find out what is available and what best suits your needs. Always remember when buying outdoor clothing and equipment, it pays to buy the best – don't skimp – because your life could depend on it.

**www.berghaus.com** Outdoor clothing, rucksacks, footwear

**www.coleman.com** Everything you need for the camp kitchen and campsite

**www.kathmandu.com.au** Outdoor clothing, rucksacks

**www.lowealpine.com** Outdoor clothing, rucksacks, boots

**www.optimus.se** Stoves

**www.trangia.se** Stoves

## PICTURE CREDITS


The publisher would like to thank the following photographers and picture agencies for their contributions:

Andrew Cox pages 13, 133 Chris Fryer pages 114–5 Getty Images pages 38, 141 Mats Hogberg pages 2, 8, 16, 21, 28, 32, 34, 37, 47, 50, 57, 63, 64, 69, 73, 76, 79–80, 83, 87, 88, 92, 96, 99, 104, 107, 111, 114, 117, 124, 129, 131, 139 Amanda Leung pages 67, 91, 125, 127 NIAC pages 1, 27, 41, 135 Photonica page 31 Gill Nisbet pages 11, 50–1, 64–5, 76–7, Tracy Timson pages 23, 24, 113 Trail magazine pages 15, 18, 54, 92–3 www.shutterstock.com 69, 74, 103, 112, 127. Cover images: Front (counterclockwise from top): Gill Nisbet, Photonica, www.shutterstock.com, NIAC. Back (top to bottom): www.shutterstock.com, www.shutterstock.com, www.shutterstock.com, Mats Hogberg

# Index